To Keep or Not to Keep

Why Christians Should Not Give Up Their Guns

Timothy Baldwin, J.D.

and

Chuck Baldwin, D.D.

Library of Congress Cataloging-in-Publication Data

Timothy Baldwin, J.D. and Chuck Baldwin, D.D.

To Keep or Not To Keep: Why Christians Should Not
Give Up Their Guns
ISBN 978-0-9888988-0-6
1. Current Affairs 2. Religious Studies
Library of Congress copyright pending

Contact the authors:

Timothy Baldwin, J.D.
PO Box 1520
Kalispell, Montana 59903
tim@libertydefenseleague.com
order@romans13truth.com

Chuck Baldwin, D.D.
PO Box 10
Kila, Montana 59920
www.chuckbaldwinlive.com

You can order these authors' work at
www.romans13truth.com and
www.chuckbaldwinlive.com.

ACKNOWLEDGMENTS

Scripture quotations are taken from the following translation: King James Version (kjv), courtesy of Sovereign Grace Publishers.

Greek and Hebrew translation and definitions are attributed to resources provided by *E-Sword*, Version 9.6.0, Copyright © 2000-2011, Rick Meyers, P.O. Box 1626, Franklin, TN 37065, United States of America, www.e-sword.net, which uses Strong's Exhaustive Concordance by James Strong, S.T.D., LL.D., 1890. These authors highly recommend this product. It is a valuable tool for scriptural study.

The source of all bible commentaries by Matthew Henry's Commentary on the Whole Bible is *E-Sword*, Version 9.6.0, Copyright © 2000-2010, Rick Meyers, P.O. Box 1626, Franklin, TN 37065, United States of America, www.e-sword.net. An additional source for Matthew Henry's Commentaries on the Whole Bible is, Thomas Scott, Matthew Henry, William Jenks, *The Comprehensive Commentary on the Holy Bible*, (Brattleboro Typographic Co., 1837). The authors reference this source in the Endnotes as "Matthew Henry, commenting on (verse)."

The authors give a special thanks to:

Golden Ratio Media, LLC (www.goldenratiomedia.com) for their outstanding graphic design work for this book.

Jarod Grubb, chief editor of The Kalispell Times, for helping to edit this book.

ABOUT THE AUTHORS

Timothy Baldwin

Timothy Baldwin, born in 1979, is Chuck Baldwin's youngest child. Timothy married Jennifer in November 2007. He and Jennifer have three children, Abigail, William and Justin.

Timothy has a unique desire to study principles of theology and politics and is formally educated in the areas of law, jurisprudence, and political philosophy.

Timothy graduated from the University of West Florida (UWF) with a Bachelor of Arts degree in 2001, where he majored in English and minored in Political Science. From UWF, Timothy attended Cumberland School of Law at Samford University in Birmingham, Alabama and graduated with his Juris Doctorate degree in 2004.

Timothy was licensed to practice law in Florida from 2004 to 2011 and is a former Florida Assistant State Attorney. He is currently licensed to practice law in Montana and practices at the Lerner Law Firm (www.lernerlawmt.com) in the city of Kalispell. Timothy handles a wide variety of cases.

Timothy (unsuccessfully) ran for Montana State House District 4 during 2012 as a Republican. He is the webmaster of www.libertydefenseleague.com and www.romans13truth.com. He has authored scores of political science articles, which have been published in various forums throughout America. Timothy gives public lectures periodically and has appeared on many radio talk shows.

Timothy is the author of *Freedom For A Change*, which is an extensive treatise on freedom and government from an Enlightenment Period perspective. He is also the co-author of *Romans 13: The True Meaning of Submission* (www.romans13truth.com).

Chuck Baldwin

Chuck Baldwin, born in 1952, is the son of Edwin and Ruth Baldwin; husband to Connie Baldwin and father to Sarah, Chris and Tim; grandfather to Emily, Jay, Amy, Charlie, James, Jeb, Abigail, William and Justin.

Growing up in small-town La Porte, Indiana, Chuck gave his heart to Jesus Christ at a young age, thanks to a loving Christian mother. Chuck gave his life to the gospel ministry when he was a teenager and initially attended Bible college at Midwestern College in Pontiac, Michigan and then later graduated from what is now Liberty Bible Institute at Liberty University in Lynchburg, Virginia. He received honorary doctorate degrees from two Christian colleges: Christian Bible College in Rocky, Mount, North Carolina, and Trinity Baptist College in Jacksonville, Florida. At age 23, Chuck and his wife, Connie, moved to Pensacola, Florida and founded Crossroad Baptist Church in 1975, pastoring there for 35 years.

Throughout Chuck's ministry, he has been involved in various points of life which concern law, society and politics; including being the Florida Executive Director for the Moral Majority, hosting *Chuck Baldwin Live* radio talk show for 8 years, 2 of which were syndicated nationally, writing weekly nationally-syndicated columns for over a decade, to name a few. Chuck was also the Presidential candidate on the Constitution Party ticket in 2008 and the Vice Presidential candidate for the same in 2004.

Chuck retired from Crossroad Baptist Church and moved to Kalispell in 2010, Montana. Chuck started a new ministry called *Liberty Fellowship* (www.libertyfellowshipmt.com) in Kalispell, which is not a 501(c)(3) entity and emphasizes biblical principles concerning law, society, and government and Christians' role in those regards. Chuck continues to articulate the issues affecting the lives of the people in America and across the world.

CONTENT

INTRODUCTION

The Context

Gun control laws are being proposed and enacted in the United States that are reducing the citizens' right to keep and bear arms to little more than a hobby. For many, the fundamentals of self-defense seem less than a by-thought to the discussion. For others, they do not know the fundamentals of self-defense, or could not care less. In addition, opposition to fundamental notions of self-defense is coming from non-government entities like the United Nations. "The United Nations and some non-governmental organizations have declared that there is no human right to self-defense or to the possession of defensive arms."[1] The issue is reaching a head today. Will Christians be prepared to answer correctly?

Proponents of eliminating America's traditional notions of self-defense say that the government must "require that a license enumerate 'specific purposes' for which a gun could be used."[2] In other words, one would need a special purpose license from the government to, say, hunt. Another license would be needed to, say, keep a gun in one's home. Included within this kind of regulation, the government would have the power to decide what kind of gun one needs for that special license and how many rounds of ammunition to go with that gun. Bottom line: gun possession would be completely and absolutely controlled by government.

Gun opponents have been highly successful in disarming the citizenry of other nations. So the threat in America is real, not just theoretical. If something does not seriously change in the attitude of Americans, our future looks similar to those who have lost meaningful and free gun possession. Unfortunately, this kind of self-defense-rejecting philosophy is becoming prevalent in America. But only one philosophy will ultimately prevail. The philosophy that succeeds will determine between two very different futures.

Fittingly, much has been written about the citizens' right to keep and bear arms guaranteed by the Second Amendment to the Constitution of the United States of America (hereinafter "Second Amendment"). Authors have largely explored whether the Second Amendment guarantees the *individual's* right to keep and bear arms or only the State's right to maintain a militia, which is an important issue.

But what does a constitutional right matter to a Christian who believes Scriptures command him to obey the government no matter what? And what does a constitutional right matter to a Christian who believes Scriptures command him to obey laws that remove meaningful self-defense against criminal and tyrant? Christians that believe God commands him to give up his guns where the law commands apparently need further persuasion that such a law is not only unconstitutional but also opposed to Scriptures. That is where this book becomes relevant.

The Response

For the purposes of persuasion, these authors analyze Scriptures and sound methods of interpretation to justify the conclusion that Scriptures support man's right to keep and bear arms; and as such, Christians must not give up necessary and proportional means of self-defense.

These authors show that Scriptures confirm the right of self-defense and provide as comprehensive and digestible proof as possible. The desired result is that a Christian can confidently rely on Scriptures to support his right of self-defense. This is an important premise to understand because where there is a *right* of self-defense, there is a *duty* to preserve and protect it.

These authors believe that "trusting is doing". One shows his faith through his work, not through his indifference.[3] "Surrendering all to Jesus" has absolutely nothing to do with giving up the rights and means God gifted man with to provide for and protect himself. Unless you think God will provide you a living, food, and shelter when you fail or refuse to work,[4] you should understand that protection of the innocent is a matter of *action, responsibility* and *duty*.

The Direction

Chapter 1 addresses who has the burden of proving the issue and the standard of proof that should be used in this attempt. The burden and the standard of proof should be understood prior to reading Chapters 2 and 3 so one will know how to view the evidence. Chapter 1 shows that self-defense rejecters hold the burden of proof and that this burden is high (the authors refer to those who claim Scripture denies the right of self-defense as "self-defense-rejecters").

Chapter 2 addresses important tools to interpret Scriptures relative to the issue. These tools should be used in conjunction with the discussion in Chapter 3. Given the principles discussed in Chapter 2, one should see how self-defense rejecters fail to meet their burden of proof.

Chapter 3 addresses specific arguments and rebuttals. In light of the methods of interpretation in Chapter 2, these authors further explain what Scriptures teaches about common arguments self-defense rejecters use and shows how self-defense is confirmed in both Testaments.

Chapter 4 addresses the elements of meaningful self-defense and how they apply today. It explains that *necessity* and *proportionality* are required and shows what that means. These authors conclude that these elements require that Christian citizens in America must not give up their guns, especially semi-automatic rifles.

The Conclusion summarizes the preceding chapters and shows why self-defense rejecters fail to meet the burden of proof, and as such, Christians can be confident that Scriptures support the right and imposes the duty of self-defense and must act accordingly.

Throughout this book, there is reference to natural law, natural right, self-defense, self-improvement and self-preservation. Each of these concepts is based on the same idea and is interconnected. To help one understand the concept, Figure 1 below demonstrates that self-defense and self-improvement rest on the natural law of self-preservation and that life requires all three elements.

Fig. 1 – Natural Law Diagram

CHAPTER 1

The Burden and Standard of Proof

This book concerns a simple yet profound issue. Does Scripture support or deny the right of self-defense; and thus, should Christians protect that right even in the face of government opposition? Like determining a factual dispute, disputes concerning the law (i.e. interpretation of words) have methods of determining the better interpretation.[5]

Our judicial systems require the same kind of burden and standard to prove a matter to a judge or jury. Without this application, our judicial system would have no sound basis of determining any factual or legal dispute. The same concept applies to every individual's decision supporting or denying their right to self-defense in accordance with Scriptures.

The following standards have been universally accepted in soundly determining both fact and law: (1) who bears the *burden of proof* and (2) what is the *standard of proof*. These are addressed below and are applied to our issue.

Burden of Proof

The burden of proof is the responsibility of proving a claim. By analogy, a person making accusation against a person for, say, breach of contract, holds the burden of proving that claim. Likewise, where the government accuses a person of committing a crime, the government bears an even heavier burden to prove the claim.

On an issue like self-defense, those attempting to change the status quo of God's creation hold the burden of proof, and that burden is heavy. Moreover, there is a presumption that self-defense rejecters are incorrect because of the following reasons:

> 1) Self-defense is the most fundamental of all human rights;[6]
>
> 2) The Old Testament supports self-defense and even requires it;[7]
>
> 3) Jesus did not come to destroy the Old Testament or Natural Law;[8]

If the New Testament must rid Christians of self-defense, it follows that self-defense existed prior to that time and was a fundamental right. Consequently, to violate the law of self-defense would pervert what God taught about justice. Therefore, answering the question, "Doth God pervert judgment? or doth the Almighty pervert justice",[9] rests on self-defense rejecters, not self-defense supporters.

Standard of Proof

To determine the standard of proof, one must take into account the "nature and significance of the factors that bear on the determination of a text's meaning [and] specify the total weight or magnitude of evidence needed to establish the meaning of a given text in a given context."[10] There are three essential factors in making this determination: identify the *admissibility*, *significance*, and *magnitude* of the evidence.

Consequently, these questions must be answered: (1) what counts as evidence of the greatest probability, (2) how much significance should be given to that evidence, and (3) how much evidence must one have to justify a particular claim and completely exclude the opposite claim.[11] These factors are addressed below.

Admissibility of Evidence

If a person wants to prove something, he has to provide evidence. The evidence must be *relevant* to the claim. Evidence is *relevant* when it is "logically connected and tending to prove or disprove a matter in issue."[12] The evidence in whether or not Scriptures support self-defense is Bible verses, both Old and New Testament.

Self-defense rejecters try to prove that God rids Christians of self-defense by arguing the Old Testament is not relevant and the New Testament creates a new Christian doctrine. However, this is incorrect. The New Testament parallels the Old Testament. Of the New Testament verses used to justify the self-defense-rejecting position, there is always Old Testament context

19

to shed light on them. The New Testament verses cannot be isolated from the Old Testament meaning. The consequence of this reality is significant in determining the issue.

Additionally, self-rejecters use early Church history to prove their claim, but this adds nothing to their argument because the determination must be based on Scriptures, not human action. The factors that affected early Christians' decisions do not define what Scriptures actually teach. If, however, human action is to be considered, then the standard is not scriptural interpretation but circumstances, culture, conditions, understanding, and the like. In this case, clearly self-defense rejecters lose as much.

<u>Magnitude of Evidence</u>

One must also know the magnitude (how much) of the evidence to choose the best conclusion.[13] Just as a jury must know how much evidence the prosecution must present to convince the jury, so one must know how much evidence is needed to decide if God has destroyed self-defense. How much evidence is needed to persuade one can be summarized as follows.

> An adequate theory of interpretation [must] specify the total weight or magnitude of evidence needed to establish the meaning of a given text in a given context. Stated simply, it does no good to have a methodology for interpreting a text unless one also knows when it is time to declare…victory or defeat and move on.[14]

The Bible reveals that how much evidence is needed to "declare victory and move on" depends on the *consequences* of the determination. This consequence-based standard has been explained this way.

> The degree of certainty, and hence the standard of proof, that people require before accepting propositions as true for particular purposes *varies with the consequences of that acceptance*...[T]here does not appear to be any sensible way to select a standard of proof *without reference to the consequences of that action.*[15]

In other words, where the consequence is great, the weight of evidence should be great. Indeed, the justice systems of the world use this biblical model and principle.[16]

Illustrating this principle, Scriptures require that for a person being charged with a capital offense (which carries the worst possible penalty), (1) the burden of proof rests on the person attempting to take away the person's liberty and (2) the standard of proof for the accuser is heightened as a result. Scriptures show that the standard requires at least two or three witnesses to the criminal act,[17] unlike other smaller crimes. Without meeting this burden and standard of proof, the accuser cannot take away one's liberty. Jesus confirms this consequence-based approach to the evidence as well when he said, "in the *mouth of two or three witnesses* every word may be established."[18] The rule is, as the risk of harm increases, the higher the standard of proof rises.

Using this scriptural standard, (1) the burden of proof is on self-defense rejecters to prove their position (just as the burden of proof is on the accuser), and (2) the standard of proof on them is heightened. If self-defense rejecters cannot meet their burden of proof, their claim fails, and one *must* find in favor of liberty and rights. This means that one must enforce self-defense and resist laws that try to take it away.[19]

Significance of Evidence

"Significance of evidence" involves the *weight of the evidence*. Since the evidence in our case involves Scriptures, this requires application of sound interpretation rules, as in any other work of literature. One will find that the evidence self-defense rejecters use to prove their claim is not significant enough to meet their burden.

Self-defense rejecters use the New Testament almost exclusively as their "weight" of evidence because the Old Testament contradicts their position. Self-defense rejecters must presume that the New Testament sets forth a new and even contradictory standard for human behavior for their evidence to hold any significance. However, the New Testament does not set forth a new standard of human behavior relative to fundamental duties of man. Jesus and the New Testament use the Old Testament to prove Christian ideas and advance them. Moreover, the New Testament increases the focus of protecting those who cannot protect themselves.

Given these realities, self-defense rejecters lose all significance relative to their New Testament "proof". The significance of the New Testament evidence outweighs self-defense rejecters' claims and actually makes them impossible.

CHAPTER 2

Interpreting Scriptures

Scripture reveals that one must understand its "true sense" to apply it correctly. Contrary to the way many apply the Bible, it takes a lot of study and practice to understand and apply the true sense of the Word.[20] Theology itself is a science, "a product of reason".[21] Some Christians erroneously believe that faith is the main factor in understanding truth. However, "feeling must become intelligent before it is truly religious."[22] Putting faith in falsehood is dangerous to society, especially concerning self-defense.[23]

Scriptural issues that do not have such a large impact on life may permit lenience in accepting various conclusions. Thus, we may "take [those verses] in some variety of interpretation."[24] However, such is not the case with self-defense because of its great consequences. So, what is the *best* conclusion?[25] To answer the question soundly, interpretation maxims (or rules) must be used, because "no scripture is of any private interpretation",[26] meaning there are sound maxims created through the light of reason and Scriptures. They include:

1) The greater prevails over the lesser.[27]

2) When a law is susceptible of two interpretations—one in favor of natural right and the other against it—the one in favor of natural right must be adopted.[28]

3) An interpretation must be reasonable, not absurd.[29]

These interpretation maxims are discussed below in specific context of the right of self-defense.

Maxim 1: The Greater Prevails Over the Lesser

The Bible is a book of principles more than a book of rules.[30] It is a "lamp unto my feet, and a light unto my path".[31] The light of Scriptures is meant for man's improvement, not his destruction. Contrary to God's plan, some choose darkness to harm others. Likewise, some foolishly choose darkness and are harmed by oppressors.[32] The light of God's law is designed to prevent both of these evils. It has been said,

> Scripture is not a complete code of rules for practical action, but an enunciation of principles, with occasional precepts by way of illustration. Hence we must supplement the positive enactment by the law of being—the moral ideal found in the nature of God.[33]

Scriptural principles show that where something is true in the greater, it is true in the lesser.[34] In other words, if "A" is a greater truth than "B", then "B" must be viewed with the greater truth in mind so that one does not destroy the truth of "A". This method of interpretation is applied throughout Scriptures and was observed this way:

> Paul's injunction to women to keep silence in the churches (1 Cor. 14:35; 1 Tim. 2:11,12) is to be interpreted by the larger law of gospel equality and privilege (Col. 3:11). Modesty and subordination once required a seclusion of the female sex which is no longer obligatory. Christianity has emancipated woman and has restored her to the dignity which belonged to her at the beginning.[35]

Take for example that Proverbs 12:10 (kjv) shows a wise man "regardeth the life of his beast". Since humans are greater than animals, man's duty towards humans requires more than "regarding" (meaning, not to unjustly harm); it requires protecting humans. Jesus demonstrated this principle of scriptural interpretation too in Matthew 12:11-12 (kjv) when he said,

> What man shall there be among you, that shall have one sheep, and if it fall into a pit on the sabbath day, will he not lay hold on it, and lift it out? How much then is a man better than a sheep?

Jesus' illustration can be extended further. If man has a duty towards man in general (the lesser), he has a greater duty to his family (by relation) and those who cannot help themselves (by circumstance).[36]

Indeed, the New Testament promotes the law of protection and preservation for beasts. "For it is written in the law of Moses, Thou shalt not muzzle the mouth of the ox that treadeth out the corn. Doth God take care for oxen?"[37] How absurd is the claim that the New Testament rejects this same law of protection for man. Does God regard oxen more than man? The following sections show that God regards man more than animals and ordains their self-defense.

Law of Sabbath v. Law of Necessity

When Jesus began his public ministry, the Pharisees accused Jesus and his disciples of breaking the Sabbath. The Pharisees said to Jesus, "Behold, why do they on the sabbath day that which is not lawful?"[38] This accusation carried the punishment of death under Jewish law, so it was very serious. Jesus did not cower but took the opportunity to reveal God's purpose for man and the proper method of interpreting law. Jesus explained that there is a higher law than even the Sabbath—the law of Necessity.

Jesus justified his and his disciples' law-breaking actions by explaining the law of necessity. He said, "the sabbath was made for man, and not man for the sabbath",[39] and

> Have ye never read what David did, when he had need, and was an hungred, he, and they that were with him? How he went into the house of God in the days of Abiathar the high priest, and did eat the shewbread, which is not lawful to eat but for the priests, and gave also to them which were with him?"[40]

Jesus explanation is significant for these reasons: (1) David was only a man and equally bound to obey the law as a common man; (2) to comply with the Sabbath law meant God would bless you with the throne of David;[41] (3) the Sabbath was sacred;[42] (4) the Sabbath was to be strictly construed, not liberally so as to "pollute" it;[43] (5) to violate it was a horrific evil;[44] and (6) others were sentenced to death in the Old Testament for slightly and arguably unintentionally violating this law.[45]

When the Pharisees accused Jesus of violating God's law, they demonstrated a method of interpreting Scriptures that did not consider the greater parts of the law that encompass the smaller parts. In other words, they failed to "give [Scripture] its full latitude."[46] In contrast, Jesus focused on the greater law, which considered the following.

1. Other values, laws and priorities created by God, including the universal law of necessity[47] and doing the greater good;[48]

2. The motives and circumstances that may necessitate violation of lesser-important laws;

3. The "appearance of evil"[49] of violating the law to be of little or no value when there was good or better things to be done;[50]

4. The "first principles" of God's creation and order and then applied reason to discern what is considered a good or evil result.[51]

Jesus' interpretation is more significant considering the kind of "good" he was performing on the Sabbath, which was nothing more than preparing a meal to eat for one day. It was a simple means to an end: eating food to minister to people. This relatively insignificant "good" demonstrates that Jesus did not consider advanced preparations for observing the Sabbath even though it conflicted with Exodus 16:23-27 (kjv).[52] In greater matters of protecting life, Jesus' method of interpretation would apply even more liberally.

Matthew Henry explained the greater law of necessity according to Jesus as follows.

> Hunger is a natural desire which cannot be mortified, but must be gratified, and cannot be put off with any thing but meat; therefore we say, It will break through stone walls. Now the Lord is for the body, and allowed his own appointment to be dispensed with in a case of distress; much more might the tradition of the elders be dispensed with. Note, That may be done in a case of necessity which may not be done at another time; there are laws which necessity has not, but it is a law to itself.[53]

Just as hunger must be satisfied through the necessity of eating, so the body must be protected through the necessity of self-defense. This law of necessity conforms to the Old Testament proverb, which says, "Be not righteous over much; neither make thyself over wise: why shouldest thou destroy thyself?"[54] One cannot interpret Scriptures in a way that destroys humanity. Put

29

another way, "if we prejudice our health by [self-denial and mortification], and unfit ourselves for the service of God, we are righteous overmuch."[55] To Jesus, obeying God meant living not destroying.[56]

Therefore, interpreting Scriptures correctly requires one to:

1) use reason of what is good and evil given the circumstances;[57]
2) understand the purpose of God's laws; and
3) understand that all law is for man's improvement *on earth*.

The Pharisees failed to do this, which Jesus highlighted when he accused them; you "strain at a gnat, and swallow a camel"[58] and "omit[] the weightier matters of the law".[59] Jesus showed through this principle that choosing to save life is a better interpretation than choosing to destroy it.

Jesus Extends Greater Good to Saving Life

Jesus extended the interpretation discussed above to saving life. The book of Luke records his teachings as follows.

> And the scribes and Pharisees watched him, whether he would heal on the sabbath day; that they might find an accusation against him. But he knew their thoughts, and said to the man which had the withered hand, Rise up, and stand forth in the midst. And he arose and stood forth. Then said Jesus unto them, I will ask you one thing; Is it lawful on the sabbath days to do

good, or to do evil? to *save life*, or to destroy it?[60]

Even though the Pharisees raised the question of healing, Jesus cut to the core matter and explained the broader principle of saving life. Jesus "put his money where his mouth was" too when he defended the adulteress whom the Pharisees desired to publically kill (Jesus knew their motive for killing was not justice but evil).[61]

Jesus' teachings on saving life mirrored well-established Jewish law, which shows how this New Testament doctrine was the same as the Old Testament. "[I]n Jewish law, there is one law which is the most important: The law of pikuach nefesh (saving lives) takes precedence over all others."[62] Matthew Henry thus noted how absurd it is to condemn one for saving life, saying,

> [Jesus] appealed to his adversaries themselves, and to the convictions of natural conscience, whether it was the design of the fourth commandment to restrain men from doing good on the sabbath day, that good which their hand finds to do, which they have an opportunity for, and which cannot so well be put off to another time...No wicked men are such absurd and unreasonable men as persecutors are, who study to do evil to men for doing good."[63]

Self-defense rejecters act in the same pharisaical manner by condemning those who resist evil. They strap on the same chains of legalism to man's demise. They claim what the Pharisees claimed: the law is greater than life. Jesus obviously rejected that interpretation of Scripture and emphatically stated, saving life is greater than following a lesser law.

The Pharisees' philosophy distorted many Jews' thinking. Prior to Jesus' ministry on earth, many Jews viewed the Sabbath so strictly that they allowed their enemies to kill them without resistance on the Sabbath because to fight is work and work was forbidden. They chose to obey the lesser at the expense of the greater. History shows, "[i]n adherence to their strict views on the observance of the Sabbath, the Jews were frequently massacred on that day without resistance".[64] Thus, when Jesus arrived and challenged the Pharisees' method of interpreting Scriptures, he answered a significant issue facing pharisaical Jews.

These self-defense-rejecting Pharisees failed to recognize that Scriptures taught the priority of seeking justice on earth so man could know God. Jeremiah 22:16 (kjv) showed them this, stating,

> Woe unto him that buildeth his house by unrighteousness, and his chambers by wrong; that useth his neighbour's service without wages, and giveth him not for his work; That saith, I will build me a wide house and large chambers, and cutteth him out windows; and it is cieled with cedar, and painted with vermilion.
>
> Shalt thou reign, because thou closest thyself in cedar? did not thy father eat and drink, and do judgment and justice, and then it was well with him? He judged the cause of the poor and needy; then it was well with him: *was not*

this to know me? saith the LORD (emphasis added).

Given that the Pharisees missed such a fundamental Old Testament doctrine, it is no wonder that they rejected Jesus' earthly ministry, which was expressly to *bring justice to the nations.*[65] The Pharisees were content that men be ruled by tyrants[66] and that men question God's justice on earth.[67] But Jesus did not follow the harmful doctrine of destroying life for the sake of following a law. Jesus preferred justice over religion.

Indeed, defending oneself is the essence of justice—the same justice that prophecy declared Jesus brought to the nations. This is why the New Testament compares Jesus to King Melchizedek, a righteous king shown in the book of Genesis, who followed the scriptural principle of self-defense. Hebrews 7:15 (kjv) makes this comparison, saying, "after the similitude of Melchisedec there ariseth another priest [Jesus]".

So, what did King Melchizedek do to deserve comparison with Jesus? Simply, he blessed Abram for recovering his abducted nephew, Lot, by force. Hebrews 7:1 (kjv) describes Abram's act, saying, he "slaughter[ed] the kings" to recover Lot, and for this act, King Melchizedek "blessed [Abram]".[68] Genesis chapter 14 records Abram's brave act, and it has been summarized as follows:

> Melchizedek blessed Abram, and also said "blessed be the most high God which hath delivered thine enemies into thy hand." Abram

gave a tithe (one-tenth) of his property to Melchizedek the priest.

When the other kings tried to bargain with Abram for the spoils of victory, Abram asked only that his allied kingdoms receive their fair share. For himself and his household and fighters, he asked only for what they had eaten.[69]

It would be a contradictory comparison to make of King Melchizedek and Jesus had Jesus condemned the same act that made this king righteous. Like King Melchizedek, Jesus embodies the Great Reward given to those who protect innocent life, and Abram's protection of innocent life was well-described as follows.

In every respect, Abram was the model of the ideal Jewish fighter: he fought to save the innocent, not for material gain. He was a bold and successful commander, who caught and destroyed enemies. He was a good diplomat who built an alliance with other victims of the aggressors. A great priest blessed him for his good works of using violence to rescue innocents.[70]

Immediately "after these things", God called Abram to be the father of the faithful in Genesis chapter 15. Out of Abram's defense act, Christians "are the children of the *prophets*, and *of the covenant* which God made with our fathers."[71] Said differently, God called Abram to be the father of Christians because of his defense of Lot, and Christians are the seed of that act. To reject the universal truth of saving life rejects God's calling of all the faithful.

Scriptures show, a sign of a destroyed community is a shortage of men able to protect those, like Lot, who are unjustly harmed.[72] Abram's defense of the innocent marked what it takes for God to bless a nation. Isaiah 54:17 (kjv) states, "No weapon that is formed against thee shall prosper...*This is the heritage of the servants of the LORD* [], saith the LORD" (emphasis added). This heritage of self-defense is a key element of God's blessing upon any nation, especially those who claim to be "servants of the Lord."[73] Therefore, to "turn from their wicked ways"[74]—thus allowing God to bless a nation—means protecting life over following lesser laws.

Pompey killed the pharisaical Jews on as many Sabbath days as they desired "*until* [the Jews] modified their conviction"[75] and began defending themselves when they put this principle into practice. These Jews finally understood what biblical scholar Matthew Henry described about following the greater law of protecting life.

> To be harmless as a dove, without gall, and not to hurt or injure others, is commendable; but to be sottish [stupefied as if drunk] as a dove, without heart, that knows not how to defend herself and provide for her own safety, is a shame.[76]

Understanding that the greater prevails over the lesser convinced the Jews to defend against oppression rather than follow a law that only facilitated their destruction. Christians should understand the same, that defenseless people are a cursed and destroyed people.

35

You Cannot Please God When Your Interpretation Harms the Innocent

There are two relationships God says are eternally important, one's relationship to God and man. God places a divine quality on man's relationship with others and requires that one comply with this duty to comply with his duty to God. Put differently, if one unjustly harms another man, his act does not conform with his duty to God. Moreover, all of the law hangs on this fact.[77] Therefore, where a scriptural interpretation harms or fails to protect life, it cannot be deemed correct.

Jesus showed how failing to comply with one's duty to man violates his duty to God as well. He said,

> For I was an hungred, and ye gave me no meat: I was thirsty, and ye gave me no drink: I was a stranger, and ye took me not in: naked, and ye clothed me not: sick, and in prison, and ye visited me not. Then shall they also answer him, saying, Lord, when saw we thee an hungred, or athirst, or a stranger, or naked, or sick, or in prison, and did not minister unto thee? Then shall he answer them, saying, Verily I say unto you, Inasmuch as ye did it not to one of the least of these, ye did it not to me.[78]

Jesus showed further that where one complies with his duty to man he satisfies his duty to God. He said,

> Come, ye blessed of my Father, inherit the kingdom prepared for you from the foundation of the world: For I was an hungred, and ye gave

me meat: I was thirsty, and ye gave me drink: I was a stranger, and ye took me in: Naked, and ye clothed me: I was sick, and ye visited me: I was in prison, and ye came unto me…Inasmuch as ye have done it unto one of the least of these my brethren, ye have done it unto me.[79]

Jesus explained this law's foundation when a lawyer asked him, "Master, which is the great commandment in the law?"[80] "Jesus said unto him, Thou shalt love the Lord thy God with all thy heart, and with all thy soul, and with all thy mind. This is the first and great commandment."[81] Jesus did not stop there but likened the law of loving God to the law of loving man. He said, "the second is like unto it, Thou shalt love thy neighbour as thyself."[82] Jesus then summarized the entire Scriptures, saying, "On these two commandments hang all the law and the prophets" and "[t]here is none other commandment greater than these."[83] Based on this universal rule, it is no wonder Jesus preferred saving life over following the Sabbath.

Jesus stated no new rule of interpretation when he said this to the lawyer, which adds further light to understanding the New Testament. Leviticus 19:18 (kjv) mirrors what Jesus said, stating, "love thy neighbor as thyself"; and the Old Testament confirms throughout that one must comply with his duty to man. For example, Ezekiel 18:5-9 (kjv) explains this duty as follows.

But if a man be just, and do that which is lawful and right…[a]nd hath not oppressed any, but hath restored to the debtor his pledge, hath spoiled none by violence, hath given his bread to the hungry, and hath covered the naked with a garment;

He that hath not given forth upon usury, neither hath taken any increase, that hath withdrawn his hand from iniquity, hath executed true judgment between man and man, Hath walked in my statutes, and hath kept my judgments, to deal truly; *he is just, he shall surely live*, saith the Lord GOD.

Plainly stated, those who comply with their duties to others are just and shall live.[84] However, one who "doeth not any of those *duties*",[85] "he shall surely die; his blood shall be upon him."[86] As this verse shows, oppressors of man shall not live, but "his blood shall be upon him". This means, when he is killed for his unjust actions, it shall be his own fault,[87] not the one who killed him.

Psalm 10:2 (kjv) reveals this same concept, which says, "The wicked in his pride doth persecute the poor: *let them be taken in the devices that they have imagined*" (emphasis added). This verse declares that those who persecute the innocent should be resisted in similar force, and those who hide the oppressor are guilty of aiding their oppression.[88] It is not an overstatement to say that every free society in the world rests on these concepts. The Old Testament's teaching of one complying with his duty to man is the same as Jesus' teaching, and Jesus never contradicted the Old Testament concerning self-defense.

To ignore or shirk this earthly duty violates one's spiritual duty to God. On the same principle, where one's interpretation harms his neighbor, that interpretation is wrong, or at the least, it is impossible as a universal command.[89] Consequently, ridding Christians of self-defense and their duty of protecting that right contradicts this scriptural principle.

Maxim 2: When an interpretation is susceptible of two meanings—one in favor of natural right and the other against it—the former must be adopted.

God chose to reveal truth through written words, which requires interpretation. It is universally accepted that interpretations can be incorrect because humans are subject to error. "Since language is the medium through which truth is expressed and formulated, the invention of a proper terminology in theology, as in every other science, is a condition and criterion of its progress."[90] Scripture itself shows that interpretation can be difficult.[91] This truth affects how one must make conclusions about scriptural teachings.

Interpretation becomes much more complicated when one is reconciling seemingly conflicting ideas or organizing a large body of ideas (i.e. the Bible). Given this reality, this maxim is more than significant: where an interpretation is subject to two conclusions—one opposed to a natural right and one in favor—the *latter must be favored.*[92] This rule is compelling because of the possibility that the interpretation opposing natural right may be incorrect. One's applying an interpretation that opposes man's natural rights results in needless injury and death, like those Jews who chose to not to defend themselves on the Sabbath because it was work.

Therefore, the interpretation favoring natural right is the most rational choice in rules of interpretation. The following sections illustrate how Scriptures recognize man's natural rights.

God Created Human Nature: Preservation and Protection

The book of Genesis shows the two essential qualities God put in man: preservation and protection. God said, "be fruitful and multiply"[93] and "[w]hoso sheddeth man's blood, by man shall his blood be shed: for in the image of God made he man."[94] Naturally, if one has the right to procreate, he has the right to protect his offspring; and if one has a right to kill another person for murder, one has the right to prevent him from committing murder. These are the foundation of God's laws about human relations, and Scriptures confirm them throughout.[95]

God did not proclaim these natural laws because man needed a command to preserve or protect life, but He expressed the *blessings* of what already existed in creation.[96] The New Testament shows the importance of this natural law by showing how God's love for the Church is founded on them: "no man ever yet hated his own flesh; but nourisheth and cherisheth it, *even as the Lord the church*".[97] As man naturally preserves and protects himself, God naturally preserves and protects the Church.

Similar to explaining God's love for the Church, the New Testament explains that love for one's neighbor is founded on love for oneself. It says, "Thou shalt love thy neighbour *as thyself.*"[98] Without love for self, there is no love for one's neighbor. As Scriptures show, preservation and protection are essential parts of loving self and can never be separated. How can one love himself but not protect oneself? How can one love his neighbor and not protect him? It is impossible.

Abraham Used Natural Right to Convince God Not to Kill Innocent People

When God considered destroying the cities of Sodom and Gomorrah, Abraham did not need written laws to convince God not to kill the innocent with the guilty. Instead, he used natural law to change God's mind. Specifically, Abraham used the "right" of the innocent, saying,

> "That be far from thee to do after this manner, to slay the righteous with the wicked, that so the righteous should be as the wicked; that be far from thee: shall not the Judge of all the earth *do right*?"[99]—that is, "do [man] right".[100]

Abraham's use of man's right is very significant. Keep in mind, Abraham was talking to God: the source of all truth, whose ways are perfect.[101] Arguably, God could have killed the innocent with the guilty, and His action would be inherently right because of who God is.[102] Still, God recognizes universal right that is at least equal to His will. This truth has been recognized this way.

Could God's command make it obligatory upon us to will evil to him? If not, then his will is not the ground of moral obligation. The thing that is most valuable, namely, *the highest good of God and of the universe must be both the end and the ground*. It is the divine reason and not the divine will that perceives and affirms the law of conduct.[103]

For Abraham to appeal to man's rights to change God's mind and for God to accept this ground show that righteous actions are based upon man's rights. More than the dirt, water, and air, man's rights were the "foundations of the earth, that...should not be removed forever."[104]

Natural Rights Serve as Basis for Human Compassion

Natural rights form the basis of justice and are the root of human compassion. Additionally, justice and compassion are mutually dependent. In other words, compassion cannot exist without rights, and rights cannot exist without compassion. It is the universal nature of man that obligates each to recognize the rights of all and love them as common descendants of God's creation. Matthew Henry observed, all "descendants [come] from one common stock, and might [are] thereby be induced to love one another."[105] As such, "oppression maketh a wise man mad."[106] Oppression makes one mad where he has compassion for his neighbor, which comes from the acknowledgment of their rights.

Where one denies another man what he is due, he fails to show love as Scriptures command, which states, "Render therefore to all their dues".[107] Rendering what is due requires the admission that one has a right to expect another to act a certain way towards him—whether in nature, law or contract. The source of working ill towards one's neighbor is failing to recognize this right. (Note: since man is incapable of always acting pursuant to this duty, government is ordained by God and instituted by man to provide a justice system for all.)

Romans 13:10 (kjv) puts the duty this way: "Love worketh no ill to his neighbour: therefore love is the fulfilling of the law." "Ill" and "harm" can only be considered wrong based upon the rights of man. Without man's rights, there is no harm, so Scriptures say. Upon this foundation the New Testament commands Christians "[t]hat no man go beyond and defraud his brother in any matter."[108] Any interpretation that works ill to one's neighbor is not love, violates God's law and rejects the basis of Jesus' redeeming man.

1 John 2:7 (kjv) thus summarizes the human element of love, saying, "I write no new commandment unto you, but an old commandment which ye had *from the beginning*." Love is an old commandment which man had from the beginning, just as man held the rights of preservation and protection from the beginning. The New Testament does not destroy the fundamental element of love that existed from the beginning any more than preservation and protection.

Scripture Confirms Natural Rights

The natural laws of procreation and protection are a blessing and ordination of God designed to create a "better state"[109] of human experience. Put shortly, God created humans not for destruction but for improvement. That people mess this up confirms the necessity of preservation and protection. This precept draws people to form society, government and law so they can "dwell in the land in safety".[110] "God's providence continues [from the beginning of Creation] so much of it to the children of men as is necessary to the safety and support of their lives."[111] Without natural rights, man would have no duty or desire to do anything but his satisfy one's own lust, which for some includes oppressing the meek.[112] To deny the right of preservation and protection rejects the most fundamental laws God and purposes of man.

The Old Testament shows throughout how man is justified in securing his natural rights of preservation and protection. It shows how these rights come from God, not government. Proverbs 29:26 (kjv) says, "Many seek the ruler's favour; but every man's *judgment cometh from the LORD*" (emphasis added). The word "judgment" (mishpât, H4941) here means man's "right, privilege, due" and is the same right Abraham uses to convince God not to destroy the innocent as discussed above. Scripture clearly states, rights do not come from government or seeking favoritism from rulers. Rather, man's rights come from the Lord and are worthy of preservation and protection. Upon this truth, God disapproves of those who "turn aside the *right* of a man"[113] and "maintain[s] [man's] right" of preservation and protection.[114] Of all man's rights, self-defense stands supreme.

Israel Resisted King Saul for Violating Natural Right

Coming from the right of preservation and protection is providing sustenance for oneself and family.[115] This states the obvious perhaps, but what would a Christian believe about a law that prevented people from eating? Perhaps it seems extremely remote, but history shows it has happened before, even in Israel.

1 Samuel 14:24 (kjv) tells of King Saul's command to the people of Israel: "And the men of Israel were distressed that day: for Saul had adjured the people, saying, *Cursed be the man that eateth any food until evening*, that I may be avenged on mine enemies. So none of the people tasted any food" even though food was plenty and cost them nothing, for "when the people were come into the wood, behold, the honey dropped" (verse 26). King Saul's son, Jonathan, had not heard of the king's law and ate wild honey. When the people found out, they feared what Saul would do and told him of the king's law. "Cursed be the man that eateth any food this day" (verse 28). By this time, the "people were faint" (verse 28) for lack of food, and they needed this food to defend themselves against their enemies. Why else does one need food except to sustain his life? Thus, the king's law was atrocious because they were engaged in self-defense for their nation.

Still, the king deprived the people of the most necessary element of life, and he did so based upon his religious belief. 1 Samuel 14:37 (kjv) reveals, "And Saul asked counsel of God, Shall I go down after the Philistines? wilt thou deliver them into the hand of Israel?" Saul's interpretation of God's will for him as a king and as a nation was erroneous, however, because "[God] answered him not." Jonathan found the king's law shameful because not only did the law violate the most basic right but also it prevented the people from being "enlightened" through its consumption. "Then said Jonathan, My father hath troubled the land: see, I pray you, how mine eyes have been enlightened, because I tasted a little of this honey" (verse 29).

Later, the king discovered that his son had eaten in violation of his law. King Saul declared, "though it be in Jonathan my son, he shall surely die" (verse 39). However, when *the people* learned of this, they decried the king's pronouncement and opposed him. The people stood up, and the king backed down. The story goes:

> And the people said unto Saul, Shall Jonathan die, who hath wrought this great salvation in Israel? God forbid: as the LORD liveth, there shall not one hair of his head fall to the ground; for he hath wrought with God this day. So the people rescued Jonathan, that he died not (verse 45).

Could a more egregious law and punishment be forced upon a people—to deny them food—during time of war—to defend themselves? The people who decried King Saul and his law did so based on the most solid and convicting grounds. Their knowledge of Creation led them to reject the king's interpretation of God's will that supposedly denied the people of their natural right of protection and preservation and to invoke man's natural right. More than being denied food, where one's life is being denied, his rightful response is to defend it.

The Anti-Christ Denies Natural Right

King Saul's command to deny people food is not the only example where man attempts, through law, to deprive others of a natural right. The book of Revelation reveals the acts of the Anti-Christ—those acts that Christians claim to despise and resist "lest they be deceived"[116]—and how he attempts to rule the nations through destroying natural right. Revelation 13:16-17 (kjv) says this about the oppression of the Anti-Christ,

> And he causeth all, both small and great, rich and poor, free and bond, to receive a mark in their right hand, or in their foreheads: And that no man might buy or sell, save he that had the mark, or the name of the beast, or the number of his name.

Like King Saul who commanded people not eat, the Anti-Christ deprives humanity of the natural right to procure food so that no man can buy or sell without receiving the mark of the beast (i.e. accepting his authority). More than King Saul depriving Israel of food for one day, the Anti-Christ does much worse by turning man's right to obtain life's necessities into a government privilege. Matthew Henry observed his attack on man as follows.

By disfranchisement, allowing none to enjoy *natural*, civil, or municipal *rights*, who will not worship that papal beast, that is, the image of the pagan beast. It is made a qualification for buying and selling the *rights of nature*, as well as for places of profit and trust, that they have the mark of the beast in their forehead and in their right hand, and that they have the name of the beast and the number of his name.

It is probable that the mark, the name, and the number of the beast, may all signify the same thing - that they make an open profession of their subjection and obedience to the [Anti-Christ], which is receiving the mark in their forehead, and that they oblige themselves to use all their interest, power, and endeavour, to promote [his] authority, which is receiving the mark in their right hands.[117]

God did not bless human life in the book of Genesis for Jesus later to command Christians to lie down as slaves of men and to give up self-defense, which is the only method God provides man to preserve and protect life.[118]

As God Himself reveals, the mark of not being the slaves of men is that they be armed, for when God led the people of Israel out of Egypt he made sure they *"went up armed out of the land of Egypt"*[119] as free people. "[A] distinctive feature of a free man is that he possesses arms, and a distinctive feature of a slave is that he does not."[120] Thus, their possession of swords literally "marked the beginning of political self-rule by the Hebrews and their spiritual liberation."[121] God expects people to protect themselves and will not use the power of miraculous plagues to do what people should be doing for themselves.

The book of Revelation shows that the Anti-Christ will attempt to destroy man's natural right of contract, which is used to preserve and protect man's life; and he will, like the Egyptian oppressors, mark man with the mark of slavery. As we know, anti-Christ types have existed since the beginning of time,[122] and they deserve resistance[123] like Cain "who was of that wicked one, and slew his brother".[124] If one is of the Wicked One because he oppresses others, he must be treated like the Wicked One, not submitted to as if he is the God of Creation. Did not the first commandment God gave to Moses state to have no other gods before man?[125] To submit to a person of the Wicked One and acting as the Wicked One like one would submit to God is blasphemy and idolatry. In summary, instead of choosing to destroy natural rights through scriptural interpretation, one is required to preserve man's natural rights and thus God's blessing of life which He ordained at Creation.

Maxim 3: The Interpretation Must Be Reasonable, Not Absurd

The New Testament says that God created man to use his reason to discern good and evil.[126] Implicit in this rule of reason is that one must understand the *nature of his decision* along with *its consequences* to himself, his family and his neighbor. Scriptures says that the distinguishing feature between animals and man is man's ability to (1) understand and seek justice, (2) discern the consequences and nature of their actions and

(3) avoid injustice.[127] More than a distinguishing feature, the ability to reason is man's glory.[128] Put simply, it "is a credit to religion when men of honesty are *men of sense.*"[129]

Unreasonable people and their damage to others must be avoided.[130] The same rule applies to *unreasonable* interpretations. The word, "unreasonable", is used two different ways in the New Testament: it means "out of place, improper, injurious, wicked" (G824, atopos) and "irrational, brutish" (G249, alogos). These definitions show one how to determine when interpretations are unreasonable.[131]

God Expects Man to Act More Justly Than Animals

The book of Proverbs states, the mark of a wise man is "to understand a proverb, and the interpretation".[132] Jesus said the same: "whoso readeth, let him understand."[133] Proverbs are given to protect and improve life. Those who do not follow the most fundamental notions of morality suffer the consequences. The plainest example of this is when oppressors violate man's most fundamental right— preservation and protection.[134] A rule that ignores this truth only promotes brutish evil.

Consider the roe and ant, says Scripture.[135] Consider that the animals "give suck to their young ones".[136] Consider that animals provide protection to their young. These are but the basics of preservation. What kind of doctrine supposes that humans must let the weak, innocent and fatherless be killed by evil men without resistance? Behold, "people [are] cruel"[137] who hold such an interpretation of "God's will". It is absurd to conclude that God revealed proverbs to man only to later impose rules for their destruction.[138]

God Requires Protection and Improvement

God designed man for preservation and improvement.[139] The Lord Himself is "for the [human] body",[140] commands that we care for it,[141] and redeemed it to Himself[142]—all for our improvement. God did not create and save man—from being "slaves to sin" to being "sons of God"[143]—for Christians to become the slaves of tyrants. The principles of protection and improvement was forever established when God made man in His image,[144] and they were reconfirmed when He gave Jesus for man.[145]

From the beginning, God established basic precepts for all humanity to protect and improve their condition.[146] Man's forming society and government extends and strengthens that purpose. Leviticus 20:25 (kjv) reveals, Israel and their civil laws were formed so "that the land...spue you not out" by natural elements and enemies.[147] By scriptural definition, this human condition requires the defense of the innocent and delivering them from oppressors.[148] The following verses show this principle.

- He shall judge the poor of the people, he shall save the children of the needy, and shall break in pieces the oppressor. Psalm 72:4 (kjv).

- Defend the poor and fatherless: do justice to the afflicted and needy. Psalm 82:3 (kjv).

- The LORD will destroy the house of the proud: but he will establish the border of the widow. Proverbs 15:25 (kjv).

- He that oppresseth the poor to increase his riches, and he that giveth to the rich, shall surely come to want. Proverbs 22:16 (kjv).

- Remove not the old landmark; and enter not into the fields of the fatherless. Proverbs 23:10 (kjv).

- Thus saith the LORD; Execute ye judgment and righteousness, and deliver the spoiled out of the hand of the oppressor: and do no wrong, do no violence to the stranger, the fatherless, nor the widow, neither shed innocent blood in this place. Jeremiah 22:3 (kjv).

These are earthly duties with earthly promises, and vice versa. They must be accomplished on earth for man's protection and improvement. Otherwise, they are hollow and meaningless. Scriptural interpretations that destroy this fundamental part of human existence are unreasonable.

CHAPTER 3

Scriptural Comparatives

of the Right to Keep Arms

It may be generally stated that the Bible teaches submission to government where it is a "terror to evil" and a "minister to thee for good".[149] But Scripture does not command submission to a law that criminalizes things fundamental to man's preservation and protection,[150] just like Israel did not allow King Saul to punish Jonathon for eating. Put another way, there may be a presumption that man should submit to government because of the alternatives of hardship and injustice that result from living in state-of-nature anarchy, but that presumption is *rebuttable* where the law destroys the most fundamental duty of man: preservation and protection. Thus, man must oppose any law that takes away the natural right and means of self-defense.

The core of making this determination is the matter self-defense. Where government criminalizes the means of self-defense against the criminal and tyrant, one cannot claim that such government is ordained of God and worthy of absolute submission. Self-defense rejecters foolishly promote a doctrine that not only commands submission to an evil government but also encourages tyrants to strip man of the rights God gave him for his preservation and protection.

The following analyzes the verses that are typically used by self-defense rejecters to justify their claim. There are variations of these, but the essence of the verses are (1) "rejoice in persecution", (2) "if you live by the sword, you'll die by the sword", (3) "resist not evil", and (4) "do not render evil for evil". Each argument is discussed separately below.

Argument 1: "Rejoice in Suffering"

An often-used support for self-defense rejecters is the doctrine of "rejoicing in suffering". Self-defense rejecters describe this as purely a New Testament doctrine to add weight to their claim. They refer to the sufferings of the early Church and claim the Christian's instruction on the subject of resistance to self-defense-rejection laws comes from their pacifism. As shown below, these arguments are erroneous.

"Rejoice in Suffering" is an Old Testament Doctrine

Classifying the doctrine of "rejoice in suffering" as purely New Testament provides self-defense rejecters a convenient way to reject the Old Testament examples of Christian faith[151] and establish a new order for Christian behavior. To them, it distinguishes the way God recognized the right and duty of self-defense in the Old Testament from the way Christians in the New Testament supposedly have the duty of letting criminals and tyrants oppress them. However, self-defense rejecters ignore the expressed parallels of this doctrine in both Testaments, which show it is not a new doctrine and thus does not destroy self-defense.

Jesus equates Christian persecution with Old Testament persecution. He said in his Sermon on the Mount, "Rejoice, and be exceeding glad: for great is your reward in heaven: *for so persecuted they the prophets which were before you.*"[152] These prophets include every Christian father that Hebrews chapter 11 exalts for exercising self-defense and Moses who defended the Hebrew slave. Jesus' comparison of both Testaments shows how man's earthly relationships are the same in both Testaments, which include the right of self-defense.

Jesus explained this universal standard of preventing injustice on earth when he stated,

> Ye are the salt of the earth: but if the salt have lost his savour, wherewith shall it be salted? it is thenceforth good for nothing, but to be cast out, and to be trodden under foot of men.[153]

Salt, in all of its metaphorical applications, is an earthly quality for earthly good to prevent oppression. Jesus called Christians to serve this earthly good and ordained government for this purpose as well. Those who do not oppress others and defend the oppressed are the salt on earth so that people not "be trodden under the foot of men". They are "ministers to thee for good".

Like Jesus, James 5:10 (kjv) likens Christian suffering with Christian forefathers, saying, "Take, my brethren, the prophets, who have spoken in the name of the Lord, for an example of suffering affliction, and of patience." This verse shows that the Christian model for "rejoicing in suffering" is the Old Testament.[154] The specific prophet the writer of James uses is Job. James 5:11 (kjv) says,

> Behold, we count them happy which endure. Ye have heard of the patience of Job, and have seen the end of the Lord; that the Lord is very pitiful, and of tender mercy.

Job suffered many inflictions, which included his servants being killed by criminals.[155] Yet, Job did not teach the kind of suffering self-rejecters propose. Job rather expressed the rightful use of the sword, saying, "Be ye afraid of the sword: for wrath bringeth the punishments of the sword, that ye may know there is a judgment."[156] The wrath that brings punishment of the sword is not limited to government, but it includes the sword of individuals who oppose the kind of criminals that killed Job's servants.

Suffering may be a reality forced upon innocent people. However, this does not mean God desires they suffer or expects them to do nothing to protect themselves. God desires that people live in peace and happiness—individually as well as politically.[157] The book of Lamentations paints this picture clearly.

> [God] doth not afflict willingly nor grieve the children of men. To crush under his feet all the

prisoners of the earth, To turn aside the right of a man before the face of the most High, To subvert a man in his cause, *the Lord approveth not. Who is he that saith, and it cometh to pass, when the Lord commandeth it not?*[158]

Of course, if there is any question about what Jesus taught relative to self-defense, he revealed how one should interpret his teachings. He said, "Think not that I am come to destroy the law, or the prophets: I am not come to destroy, but to fulfil."[159] This law absolutely includes the law of self-defense.

Given the host of Old Testament laws and examples supporting the right and duty of preservation and protection, it is quite the contradictory theory to say that Jesus destroyed those laws when he himself declared he did not. Jesus reiterated Old Testament law because they are the foundation of Christian principles. As such, Jesus declared that Christians who "shall do [the commandments of the Old Testament], the same shall be called great in the kingdom of heaven."[160] It is no wonder that the great Christian fathers of the Old Testament like Abraham, Moses, and David all exemplified one who firmly believes in self-defense, each of whom the New Testament praises for their acts.

"'Rejoice in Suffering' Means No Self-Defense" Is Illogical

Self-defense-rejecter logic goes: (premise 1) I should rejoice when I suffer for Jesus' sake; (premise 2) being oppressed by a criminal or tyrant is suffering for Jesus' sake; (conclusion) therefore, I should never prevent them from attacking me because if I do, I am not rejoicing in suffering. This logic is flawed for many reasons and contradicts Scriptures.

In truth, the New Testament teaches the opposite of this logic. Take the example of Moses. Hebrews 11:24-27 (kjv) says that Moses' choice of defending the Hebrew slaves instead of remaining in Pharaoh's family was *suffering for Christ*. These verses reveal:

> By faith Moses, when he was come to years, refused to be called the son of Pharaoh's daughter; *Choosing rather to suffer affliction* with the people of God, than to enjoy the pleasures of sin for a season; *Esteeming the reproach of Christ* greater riches than the treasures in Egypt: for he had respect unto the recompence of the reward. By faith he forsook Egypt, *not fearing the wrath of the king*: for he endured, as seeing him who is invisible.

Significantly stated, the Apostle Paul described Moses' defense act as suffering for Jesus *even though* Jesus' earthly existence began years in the future. This means defense of the innocent is a universal principle that goes beyond dispensations, and it reveals how Jesus justified Moses' act under New Testament doctrine.

Given that self-defense derives from an act of love, this conclusion should not be curious given the New Testament's emphasis on loving one's neighbors as himself. Where a person is forced to defend others, he defends out of sacrifice and love in protecting "the least of these".[161] Clearly, love is the greatest of all Christian attributes and commandments.[162] Equally clear, a person risking his life to save another person's life is the greatest act of love.[163] Against such an act there is no condemnation. Moreover, there is only justification for that act of love, as it satisfies all the law.[164] There is nothing in either Testament to show this act of love for others is disqualified as being good.

Yes, Christians were persecuted for expressing their faith. These martyrs "cho[se] rather to suffer affliction"[165] and some "did not resist".[166] These martyrs existed before and after Jesus. However, Hebrews chapter 11 describes those faithful to God and the principles of Jesus that *did resist*. It says,

> [T]ime would fail me to tell of Gedeon, and of Barak, and of Samson, and of Jephthae; of David also, and Samuel, and of the prophets: Who through faith subdued kingdoms, wrought righteousness, obtained promises, stopped the mouths of lions, Quenched the violence of fire, escaped the edge of the sword, out of weakness were made strong, waxed valiant in fight, turned to flight the armies of the aliens.[167]

These models of Christian heroism are the same people Psalm 136:15-18 (kjv) describes as having "overthrew Pharaoh", "smote great kings", and "slew famous kings". The parallel between Hebrews 11 and Psalm 136 are like so many other parallels that show God ordains self-defense. Where the New Testament praises those who use self-defense, self-defense rejecters gain nothing to meet their heavy burden of proof.

Circumstances affect each person's response to the evil confronting them. There are times when resistance is futile, people are overtaken by force, and death is inevitable. Jesus put it like this: "Woe unto the world because of offences! for it must needs be that offences come."[168] Such a reality of human existence does not eliminate the justification of defending oneself and others, nor does it serve as an excuse to do nothing, as if God expects Christians to let evil people rule on earth. As Jesus put it, "Woe to that man by whom the offence cometh!"[169] Instead of causing one to surrender self-defense, knowing that evil people seek destruction of the innocent should cause a just man to take appropriate steps of protecting himself and his family,[170] "redeeming the time, because the days are evil"[171]

This duty to protect "those of his own household"[172] is clear since the New Testament declares that our bodies are not governments' but God's.[173] So when we "give unto Caesar that which is Caesar's"[174] this excludes innocent life and the means of protecting it.[175] It also excludes the right of protecting those God entrusts to our care. Psalm 127:3 (kjv) states this specifically: "Lo, *children are an heritage of the LORD*: and the fruit of the womb is his reward" (emphasis added). Indeed, one of the expressed purposes of God's giving children to man is for protection. This is obvious given the natural strength young people have. Psalm 127:4-5 says,

> As arrows are in the hand of a mighty man; so are children of the youth, Happy is the man that hath his quiver full of them: they shall not be

ashamed, but they shall *speak* with the enemies in the gate.

Given the context of this verse, the word "speak" here more likely means "subdue".[176] When children reach a point of physical and mental maturity and are able to subdue enemies in the gate, children become "a great support and defence to a family."[177]

Once again, this New Testament reality is the same presented in the Old Testament when God delivered Israel from the bondage of Egypt. God's people are not called to be slaves of men.

> [Israel's] physical exodus [from Egypt] was also a "spiritual exodus from the cosmological form of imperial rule. The sonship of god is transferred from the pharaoh to the people of Israel in immediate existence under Yahweh." Hence, a person's life belongs to God, not to the government.[178]

Only the foolish do not protect this principle of freedom exemplified in both Testaments.[179]

Using People or Scriptures?

Scriptures prove that God supports the right of self-defense. To get around this proof, self-defense rejecters point to the sufferings of the early Church at the hands of government rather than using Scriptures, supposing that early Christians had a firmer handle on Scriptures than later Christians. In so doing, they use early Christians as a lens to distort scriptural teachings regarding the right of self-defense. Contrary to the teaching of self-defense rejecters, "[t]heology...looks to the Scripture itself as its chief source of material and its final standard of appeal."[180] It is "error...making the church, and not the Scriptures, the immediate and sufficient source of religion's knowledge".[181] As Jesus said, "making the word of God of none effect through your tradition" is wrong.[182] However, if one is going to use human conduct as the benchmark for interpreting Scriptures, then many factors must be considered to reach an accurate conclusion about the Church's progress throughout history. In either case, self-defense rejecters gain no significance to their position.

Right away, as self-defense rejecters point to Church history to support their claim, the self-defense supporter trumps this argument by using the New Testament examples of Christian faith. Of those, it specifically names defenders of the innocent, as has already been discussed above. Which is more significant to persuade the Christian's belief?—whom Scriptures uses as Christian faith or whom self-defense rejecters use as Christian faith? The answer is obvious.

Is it possible that early Christians did not have the kind of knowledge and experience needed to rid themselves of tyranny? Look how long Christians have decried legalized abortions in America—for a few generations now. Does this mean abortions are God's desire for Christians and should be used to interpret Scriptures? No. Look how long Israel lived in slavery to Egypt. Were their actions the standard to interpreting God's laws? No. Noticeably, both Testaments reveal that the reason Israel stayed in slavery so long was because "they understood not".[183] What did they not understand? They neither understood that their *process of freedom* began when Moses acted in their defense by killing the taskmaster, nor did anything to help Moses. Had they stood with Moses at this time, undoubtedly God would have given them liberty. Pharaoh knew that, which is why he began killing the young male children.[184]

Notable to this story's background is that the government used baby-killing to keep Israel enslaved. Do Christians today find this kind of baby-murder to be God's will? Would a self-defense rejecter not oppose infanticide on justice alone? It appears self-defense rejecters are in a moral dilemma that cannot be reconciled with their self-defense-rejection doctrine because if a Christian cannot defend adults, then he cannot defend babies either; and what Christian holds a doctrine that permits babies to be killed without resistance? Self-defense rejecters that deny the righteousness of defending innocent children fit in Jesus' following condemnation.

> But whoso shall offend one of these little ones which believe in me, it were better for him that a millstone were hanged about his neck, and that he were drowned in the depth of the sea. Woe unto the world because of offences! for it must needs be that offences come; but woe to that man by whom the offence cometh![185]

Yes, "it must needs be that offences come" because evil people exist. No, Jesus does not command that righteous people permit evil acts like harming innocent children and other people. Those who do nothing to protect the most innocent of society can say nothing more for themselves than they aid evil. Bible scholar, Matthew Henry, says about these people, "Woe to those who help to make the times thus perilous."[186] There is no excuse and certainly no honor for self-defense rejecters to justify not defending innocent people based on an interpretation of Scriptures that is, at the very least, subject to an alternative and reasonable interpretation (i.e. the right of self-defense). If God's attribute is to deliver all oppressed,[187] why do Christians choose to work against God and help oppressors through their self-defense rejection?

Now going back to Israel's enslavement—their circumstances prior to that time may not have been ripe for revolution. But at the time Moses defended the Hebrew slave, their numbers and strength were great enough to free themselves from their needless slavery. Unfortunately for Israel, their response to Moses' courage was, "Who made thee a prince and a judge over us? intendest thou to kill me, as thou killedst the Egyptian?"[188] Their response is not only absurd but illogical. They clearly had no concept of what just cause and self-defense meant; or worse, they rejected it. Moses revealed Israel's ignorance of the most basic notion of justice (i.e. self-defense) in Acts 7:26 (kjv) when he questioned them, saying, "why do ye wrong one to another?" The reason Israel did not understand self-defense is because they did not understand God's most basic principle of morality, "Strive not with a man without cause".[189] Israel's ignorance of God's law caused them to suffer in slavery until God sent Moses back to finish what he started. Any generation will likewise suffer in slavery when they reject self-defense, because as Scripture says, "the slothful shall be under tribute."[190] Self-defense rejecters are slothful in heart, mind, and actions and voluntarily put today's Christians in a place of slavery—a place where God delivered Israel centuries ago through Moses' act of defense. How absurd.

Like the Hebrew slaves, early Christians may have believed God intended that they live in oppression, or perhaps they felt extremely incompetent to enforce the Christian principles of equality, justice and protection. Regardless, their actions do not bear rule over Scriptures. It is true, God provided "no orderly arrangement...either in nature or in Scripture"[191] of theological principles but "[gave] us truth in single threads, which we must weave into a finished texture."[192] Expounding theological principles requires time and study and is "constructed by putting together multitudinous facts which at first sight seem to have no order."[193] How Christians developed and how quickly they developed these principles is a matter of history. How Christians learn today is a matter of choice. But Scriptures show how knowledge has not always been quickly learned in a short time.[194] Gaining knowledge is the task for all Christians, and early Christians were at the biggest disadvantage for many reasons.

The difficulty of understanding the fullness of Scriptures is seen in the ministry of Nehemiah as well when even the Jewish religious leaders did not know the law. Before the people could learn the law's "true sense", the leaders had to study and enlighten their minds. Many suffered for their lack of understanding the law. In many instances, God himself had to teach them what the law meant because of their ignorance. That they suffered for lack of understanding did not glorify their ignorance, and it did not serve as the model for future generations.

This is not meant to overly criticize people who act in unintentional ignorance, for God excused ignorance too.[195] As has been observed concerning God's design for Christians,

> God's furnishing of concrete facts in theology, which we ourselves are left to systemize, is in complete according with his method of procedure with regard to the development of other sciences.[196]

History shows, the Church applied the science of knowledge to Scriptures and improved theology itself. They did not sit back and do nothing about tyranny over time. They, like Moses, improved their condition and the world's through self-defense. Springing from this, theologians became the most outspoken and unmoving advocates of the rights of man, and through their knowledge and work, these rights have become guaranteed in state constitutions across the world.

Regardless of what early Christians did or did not do, Christian Americans (who possess the combined freedom of centuries of Christian sacrifice and labor) have no excuse to be slothful, to act like enslaved-Israel, and to reject God's law of self-defense. It is shameful for self-defense-rejecter Christians, like the Israelites who ludicrously accused Moses for defending them, to bask in the sunshine of freedom and prosperity created by Christians who exercised self-defense.

A Secular Philosopher's View

In sharp contrast to the claim that Christianity rids individuals of the right to resist criminals and tyrants, secular philosophers have concluded the opposite about Christianity. George Hegel is among those most famous philosophers who saw Christianity as being the most influential cause of limiting government and increasing individual liberty. Hegel's view is significant because he sought to diminish the value of the individual and increase the "idea of the State" over the individual.

In his *Philosophy of Right*, Hegel began discussing the "idea of the State" by describing Christianity's influence on political institutions and said,

> It is about a millennium and a half since the *freedom personality began through the spread of Christianity to blossom and gain recognition as a universal principle*...of the human race...This example from history may serve to rebuke the impatience of opinion and to show the length of time that mind requires for progress in its self-consciousness.[197]

Had Hegel believed Christianity ridded people of the basic right of preservation and protection, Hegel would have heralded Christianity for increasing State power and eliminating individual right. This is evident given how Hegel described the individual's duty to "sacrifice [himself] on behalf of the state".[198] Such is a "universal duty", said Hegel.[199]

Upon the principles expressed in the New Testament, Hegel described the conflict between the individual and State and showed how all objective truth comes from the State, not from God. He said,

> If the state is confused with civil society, and if its specific end is laid down as the security and protection of property and personal freedom, then the interest of the individuals as such becomes the ultimate end of their association, and it follows that membership of the state is something optional. But the state's relation to the individual is quite different from this. Since the state is mind objectified, it is only as one of its members that the individual himself has objectivity, genuine individuality, and an ethical life.[200]

Hegel said, Christianity teaches that the object of government is the good of the individual (i.e. life, liberty and property). Indeed it does, but Hegel did not believe such a view of government is correct. Evidently, self-defense rejecters agree with Hegel and not with Scriptures because they do not believe government is designed to protect our right of self-defense.

Hegel further insulted Christianity's influence on politics, claiming that "true religion" does not conflict with government. He said, "if religion be religion of a genuine kind, it does not run counter to the state in a negative or polemical way."[201] Strangely, self-defense rejecters accept the same Hegelian conclusion; but again, Hegel thought Christianity concluded very differently. Undoubtedly, if Hegel believed Scriptures taught his version of the individual's duty to government, he would have invoked that doctrine or even Church history, but he never did.

Hegel also mocked Enlightenment Philosophy because it was based upon scriptural principles. One of the fundamental notions advanced through this philosophy was (1) people form constitutions to protect their lives, property and pursuit of happiness and (2) those constitutions must be adhered to, subject to change only by the people, not by government officials at their whim. Hegel rejected this principle advanced by Christianity and promoted a very different constitutional theory. He said,

> In our day there has come before the public an endless amount of babble about the constitution [] thanks to those who have persuaded themselves that they have the best, or even the sole, understanding of what a constitution is...And these gentlemen are convinced that they have an unassailable justification for what they say because they claim that religion and piety are the basis of all this shallow thinking of theirs. It is no wonder that this babble has made reasonable men just as sick of the words

"reason," "enlightenment," "right," &c., as of the words "constitution" and "freedom".

Blatantly put, Hegel rejected all notions advanced by the Enlightenment/Christian philosophy that a constitution must protect individual rights. (Note: Hegel shows that the way the State controls the Church is for churches to be viewed as state corporations.[202]) Ironically, self-defense rejecters give no place for what Christian principles have advanced concerning government and its purpose. Instead, they reduce Christians to lower than animal status, supposedly under a "better covenant with better promises."[203] They are perfect pawns of evil government and act as if they are doing God's bidding.

An objective observer should see that if Scriptures taught that individuals held no power to resist or influence government, then State-lovers would adore Christianity as being the world's model religion. Yet, there are no such tyrannous governments. Were self-defense rejecters' view of Scriptures true, Christianity would provide every opportunity for tyrants to control all people without fear of resistance in any form and case. Contrary to what self-defense rejecters proclaim about "God-haters kicking God out of school and removing the Bible from our children's public teaching", if Scriptures taught self-defense rejection, "God-haters" would advance Christianity everywhere and advance the submit-to-government-no-matter-what doctrine. So, why do some insist on removing God and the Bible from public life? Hegel provided his answer: because of Christianity's effect of limiting the "idea of the State" and increasing the individual rights. Simply put, self-defense rejecters and God-haters are allies in the same battle to remove individual rights from social life.

Hegel's view of Christianity differs little from government rulers when Jesus and the apostles lived. If Christianity *so clearly and expressly* taught unlimited submission to government and eliminated individual right, then government rulers would have embraced Christianity. Thus, while Jesus said, "render therefore unto Caesar",[204] the Roman government did not take his statement to mean what self-defense rejecters claim. As such, the Roman government vehemently opposed Christianity because its principles threatened political power.[205] They were right, and time proved it.

Hegel reflected what the Romans foresaw. Governments that see no threat to political power will leave those people alone. A government that destroys members of society that unconditionally submit to its absolute power destroys the source of its power. There was something more to Christianity than mystics, religion or spiritual life. It formed the principles which future Christians advanced to eventually push down the pillars of tyranny for centuries, like Samson destroying the playhouse of the wicked.[206] Therefore, if one considers human actions to determine the issue, he must look at how governments ardently opposed Christianity.

Scriptures teach that the Christian life is a matter of growth. "But grow in grace, and in the knowledge of our Lord and Saviour Jesus Christ", says 2 Peter 3:18 (kjv). The same principle of growth applies to the collective Christian life. It is dishonest to state that early

Christians had a firmer grasp of all Christian doctrines and principles than later Christians who had the benefit of combined study, time and opportunity to understand the "more sure word of prophecy".[207] Thankfully, Christians improved their knowledge of scriptural principles over time. This took generations and much blood was spilled to climb the plateaus of understanding and enlightenment. As they did, the truth of self-defense was advanced in politics and government administration, and it became guaranteed in our constitutions as a universal right. No free people ever rejected this universal truth, as the history of Israel proves.

Argument 2. "If You Live by the Sword, You Will Die by the Sword"

Contrary to what self-defense rejecters claim, Jesus' statement, "if you live by the sword, you will die by the sword", confirmed the proper use of the sword—for self-defense.

Just moments before Jesus was arrested through the betrayal of Judas, Jesus and his disciples were in the garden of Gethsemane ("garden") at night. Jesus knew the time of his crucifixion was near, but his disciples did not. While Jesus and his disciples were gathered, his enemies surrounded Jesus and his disciples. His crucifixion was only hours away, but he took the time to express the true meaning of living and dying by the sword.

After the disciples realized what was taking place in the garden, they asked Jesus, "shall we smite them with the sword?"[208] If Jesus responded, Scriptures do not record it. Either he said, yes, or he said nothing at all. Whatever his response was, Peter took it to mean he should use the sword in their defense. So, Simon Peter attacked, and Jesus did or said nothing to stop him. Peter's attempt was unsuccessful but he did cut the ear off of one. The story goes,

> Then Simon Peter having a sword drew it, and smote the high priest's servant, and cut off his right ear. The servant's name was Malchus. Then said Jesus unto Peter, Put up thy sword into the sheath: the cup which my Father hath given me, shall I not drink it?[209]

As recorded in another Gospel book, Jesus said in response:

> Then said Jesus unto him, Put up again thy sword into his place: for all they that take the sword shall perish with the sword.[210]

Self-defense rejecters argue that Jesus' statement means Christians cannot use the sword for defense purposes and must be absolutely passive even in the face of unjust attack. This interpretation is wrong.

Instructions, "Put Up Thy Sword", Did Not Prohibit Sword Possession

Notice the obvious: Jesus did not command Peter to *give up* his sword or right to use it. Peter retained possession of his sword per Jesus' instructions. Given Peter's attempt to kill them, this is no small thing.

Obviously, had Jesus taught what self-defense rejecters claim, Jesus would not have allowed Peter to walk away with his sword, and their enemies would have enforced what Jesus taught.

Jesus' instruction to Peter showed that his use of the sword was not wrong but untimely because of what Jesus had to do. Jesus said directly after he told Peter to put away his sword, "how then shall the scriptures be fulfilled, that thus it must be?";[211] "shall I not drink [of the cup which my Father hath given me]?"[212] Jesus was the only person who knew God's will for him. He thus had to explain why he told Peter to put away his sword because the circumstances warranted its use; and Jesus admitted this, saying, "Thinkest thou that I cannot now pray to my Father, and he shall presently give me more than twelve legions of angels?"[213] Since their enemies were acting as thieves and murderers in the night,[214] Jewish law justified their self-defense, and they all knew it. That was the only reason a group of men were needed to arrest Jesus. They expected a fight, and they would have gotten one were it not for Jesus' instruction to Peter.

Jesus' act was prophesized many years prior and could only be accomplished by his drinking that particular cup at that particular time. Moreover, Jesus' death was to be done only once in history by him alone.[215] So as necessary as it may have been for Peter to use the sword, it was *more necessary* that Jesus die for man so that they may have eternal life through his death.

Jesus' instruction to Peter was not a universal command to Christians to give up self-defense.

Jesus "It-is-Enough" Response to Inquiry about Number of Swords

Adding more light to the matter is how Jesus responded to his disciples when they asked him if two swords were enough after he had instructed them to buy a sword if they did not have one. Their conversation follows.

> For I say unto you, that this that is written must yet be accomplished in me, And he was reckoned among the transgressors: for the things concerning me have an end. And they said, Lord, behold, here are two swords. And he said unto them, *It is enough.*[216]

Some interpret Jesus' response to the disciples informing him that they only had two swords shows that Jesus did not really want them to possess swords. The other interpretation is that Jesus told the disciples that his discussion of possessing swords was concluded. Of the two interpretations, the latter is the most probable.

Jesus had just told his disciples that if they did not have a sword then they should sell their garments and buy one. Jesus knew that of the eleven, only two swords were present. Peter had one, and it is likely Matthew, the publican, had the other. For Jesus to immediately tell them two swords are enough is illogical and contradictory. If Jesus had not intended for all his disciples to possess swords he would not have instructed them to buy them; otherwise, his instructions would have amounted to nothing.

This interpretation is shown by the change of Jesus' conversation from swords to his approaching his end on earth. When Jesus began discussing what the Old Testament prophesied concerning his end, his disciples interrupted him and asked again about sword possession. To Jesus, there was no need to further discuss that topic. Jesus thus said, "it is enough." The disciples only had to follow his simple instructions: go buy swords if you do not have them. Therefore, the most logical interpretation of this passage is that once Jesus instructed his disciples concerning buying swords, there was no other cause for discussing his instructions. Jesus did not nullify the instructions he given only seconds prior.

"Live by the Sword-Die by the Sword" Statement Confirms Self-Defense

Jesus' statement, "they that take the sword shall perish with the sword", has two main interpretations.

(1) People who defend themselves with the sword shall perish with the sword, or

(2) People who oppress others with the sword shall perish with the sword.

Of the two, the second is the only possible choice. Jesus was very familiar with the many Old Testament references supporting the second interpretation. Jesus did not advance a concept contradicting Jewish law and destroy the Old Testament revelations that confirmed, "they that take the sword shall perish with the sword."

Exodus 22:2 (kjv) states God's law of self-defense: "If a thief be found breaking up, and be smitten that he die, there shall no blood be shed for him."[217] This, of course, follows the natural law God declared in Genesis 9:6 (kjv). "Whoso sheddeth man's blood, by man shall his blood be shed: for in the image of God made he man." More than permitting self-defense, the Torah imposed the *duty* of self-defense. Scholar, David Kopel, described God's law this way.

> [T]he Torah decreed "If he come to slay thee, forestall by slaying him." This last sentence is sometimes translated, "If someone comes to kill you, rise up and kill him first." The final sentence is not an option; it is a positive command. A Jew has a duty to use deadly force to defend herself against murderous attack.[218]

> The duty to use force to defend an innocent is based on two passages. The first is Leviticus 19:16, "you shall not stand up against the life of your neighbor." Or in a modern translation [New American Bible], "nor shall you stand idly by when your neighbor's life is at stake."

> The second passage comes from Deuteronomy and explains that if a man and a betrothed (engaged) woman have illicit sex in the city, it would be initially presumed that she consented because she could have cried out for help. But if the sexual act occurred in the country, she would be presumed to have been

the victim of a forcible rape, "For he found her in the field, and the betrothed damsel cried, and there was none to save her." The passage implies that bystanders must heed a woman's cries and come to her rescue[219]

The people of Israel and Jesus knew what living and dying by the sword meant, and it absolutely did not condemn self-defense.

If Jesus' statement meant Peter *did not* have a just cause for defense, then Peter was guilty of attempted murder and of violating Jesus' statement. Moreover, Jesus' statement contradicted Old Testament law. So, if Jesus truly meant that those who live by the sword should die by the sword, then Peter should have been killed for his action, and Jesus would have willingly allowed the soldiers to take Peter and his sword. These soldiers would and should have taken both Peter's sword and life. But they did not, because Jesus protected Peter; and Jesus protected Peter because his action was not wrong—it was only untimely.

Therefore, "[Jesus'] injunction...necessarily implies the right of self-defense; for how could they perish who take the sword unless those who are assailed defense themselves? Such view of the admonition is put beyond doubt by the passage in Revelation 13:10",[220] which states, "he that killeth with the sword must be killed with the sword." Like Revelation 13:10 and the entirety of Scriptures, Jesus' statement shows that living and dying by the sword did not prevent Christians from using self-defense. From beginning to end, the Bible supports the use of the sword to protect life.

Jesus Uses Old Testament Term to Reveal Meaning

Jesus' statement carried meaning that was defined through the Old Testament. Jesus accepted that meaning and used it to reveal truth relative to the situations he encountered. In so doing, he confirmed the right of self-defense.

The first Old Testament reference of the term "live by the sword" is found in Genesis chapter 27. This verse was written about Esau after he lost his father's birthright. Jacob (the younger brother) held the birthright and became the one through whom God blessed the nation of Israel. Recognizing what Esau lost, Isaac said to his son, "by thy sword shalt thou live, and shalt serve thy brother."[221] Isaac explained that Esau was not without his natural rights as a child of men, so Matthew Henry noted the following concerning Isaac's consolation to Esau.

> If Jacob must rule (Gen 27:29), Esau must serve; but he has this to comfort him, he shall live by his sword. He shall serve, but he shall not starve; and, at length, after much skirmishing, he shall break the yoke of bondage, and wear marks of freedom. This was fulfilled (2 Ki 8:20, 2 Ki 8:22) when the Edomites revolted.[222]

Esau may have lost the preeminence of God's Abrahamic covenant, but he did not lose the right to preserve and protect himself. In Esau's case, living by the sword was a blessing—a self-evident blessing all humanity shares. Ultimately, Esau's descendants exercised this natural right and freed themselves from tyranny by the sword.[223] Thus, in this case, living by the sword did not equate to dying by the sword as Jesus described.

The Old Testament, however, reveals a different kind of living by the sword—the kind that results in death—the kind Jesus described. Job 27:13-15 (kjv) shows this kind of living and dying by the sword as follows.

> *This is the portion of a wicked man* with God, and the *heritage of oppressors*, which they shall receive of the Almighty. If his children be multiplied, *it is for the sword*: and his offspring shall not be satisfied with bread. Those that remain of him *shall be buried in death*: and his widows shall not weep (emphasis added).

Like the Old Testament, Jesus rightly warns oppressors: if you insist on oppressing the innocent you will die by the sword like the oppressors of Edom died. "This is the portion of a wicked man", Scriptures say. It is an absurd interpretation to say Jesus condemned self-defense but not tyranny when the Old Testament proclaims the opposite.

People who use unjust violence against the innocent are rebuffed by foreign governments, domestic government, or those whom they oppress, Scriptures show. An example of when the oppressed avenge their right is described in the book of Habakkuk, which says,

> Shall they not rise up suddenly that shall bite thee, and awake that shall vex thee, and thou shalt be for booties unto them? Because thou hast spoiled many nations, all the remnant of the people shall spoil thee; because of men's blood, and for the violence of the land, of the city, and of all that dwell therein.[224]

People rightfully rise up against those that (1) spoil other nations (unjustly creating foreign enemies), (2) kill innocent people, (3) damage the land (the means through which people live), (4) put violence in the city (not enforcing just laws so people can live in peace with each other), and (5) put violence upon all that dwell in the nation. Notably, these evil acts are characteristic of Satan himself,[225] whom we are commanded to resist.[226] King David believed acting in this satanic manner deserves retribution by those harmed as well,[227] and Jesus unequivocally showed the same: those who unjustly take the sword will die by the sword. Jesus' ministry on earth was meant to prevent and remedy these evils, not advance them. How absurd is the doctrine that claims Jesus condemns the innocent for protecting the good God created.

Jesus' Instructions Opposed Roman Law

What Jesus taught on the subject is understood more clearly considering Jesus instructed his disciples to buy swords when this violated Roman law. The Jews were living under foreign rule at this time. As sub-class inhabitants to a foreign power, the government prohibited them fundamental rights. One of the most basic rights of citizenship—military sword possession—was denied them by law. The reality of this legal contest was explained as follows.

> Under Roman law, citizens had a right to carry personal arms...[However], Roman law forbade the Jews and other subject people to carry swords, under penalty of death. (Apparently, the apostles of Jesus violated this law by carrying a pair of swords.)[228]

That Jesus would instruct his disciples to buy swords when that was a capital offense under Roman law is significant. What is also notable about this is that during the years Jesus led his disciples, he knew his disciples carried swords against Roman law. Yet, he never ordered them not to carry swords. Similarly, the disciples never gave up their swords in face of the Roman law, and when Jesus told them to each buy one, they intended to obey Jesus rather than Roman law.

While Jesus had instructed his disciples not to carry swords when they mingled with the people in the beginning of ministry, this instruction was limited in time, purpose and scope. Now was the time for Jesus to teach his disciples the lesson of practical preparations in life:

> And he said unto them, When I sent you without purse, and scrip, and shoes, lacked ye any thing? And they said, Nothing. Then said he unto them, But now, he that hath a purse, let him take it,

and likewise his scrip: and he that hath no
sword, let him sell his garment, and buy one.[229]

This further shows that Jesus' previous instruction to his
disciples that they be "harmless as doves" was also
limited to their particular purpose for that time,[230] which
Jesus revealed about his own ministry.[231] Jesus'
instruction to his disciples to buy swords in contradiction
to Roman law necessarily means he accepted its rightful
use.

The Unrecorded Response of the Soldiers

What is missing from the garden story is how
Jesus' enemies responded to Peter's kill attempt.
Common sense supplies the possibilities. The *first
possibility* is that they tried to take Peter's sword but
Jesus would not let them. The *second possibility* is that
they did not try to take Peter's sword from him. The
result of either possibility reveals Jesus' view of the
right of self-defense.

Certainly these men could have dispossessed
Peter of his sword given their de facto power and ill
intent. They would have done more than take his sword
for what Peter did: they would have killed him. But they
did nothing, and Peter left with his life and sword. This
is all the more significant given Roman law prohibited
Jews (and later Christians) from possessing Roman
swords (the military weapon of that day). Therefore,
there is one reason they did not so attempt: Jesus did not
permit them.

This is evident given what happened prior to Peter's attempting to kill them. The book of John records how Jesus responded to their assault this way.

> Judas then, having received a band of men and officers from the chief priests and Pharisees, cometh thither with lanterns and torches and weapons. Jesus therefore, knowing all things that should come upon him, went forth, and said unto them, Whom seek ye? They answered him, Jesus of Nazareth. Jesus saith unto them, I am he. And Judas also, which betrayed him, stood with them. *As soon then as he had said unto them, I am he, they went backward, and fell to the ground.*[232]

Jesus' words were so forceful that it knocked his enemies to the ground. Clearly, these men knew this was no ordinary situation. Had Jesus wanted to call a league of angels to destroy these men, he could have. Jesus' enemies felt this power from Jesus' words alone.

Jesus' words to these enemies were like what was later revealed about his words being a sword to his enemies: "Repent; or else I will come unto thee quickly, and *will fight against them with the sword of my mouth.*"[233] Jesus' enemies experienced only a small portion of his sword, but it was enough to see that Jesus was not going to let them hurt or disarm his disciples.

The Roman Warrior Shows Christian Faith

Jesus' view of those who "live by the sword" is further revealed in a man Jesus said possessed more Christian faith than any person in the nation. This man was a Roman centurion—a military officer who had achieved his military rank because of his war skills. During Jesus' discussion with him, Jesus never instructed him to give up his sword or retire from military service—and this soldier was a Christian. Instead, Jesus magnified this Christian while in his capacity as a military warrior and commander-in-chief.

Jesus also accepted this soldier's comparison between the relationship of military authority and Jesus' authority.[234] As has been rightly observed, "[h]ere would have been asserted the unlawfulness of the use of arms had the Master thought it wrong."[235] Jesus always took the opportunity to pierce into matters most concerning righteousness and justice: he did so with the Pharisees, Simon Peter, the rich man, King Herod and anyone else who needed it. Yet in this case, Jesus not only condemns him not, but also praises him above all Christians in Israel.

Additionally, if Jesus' command of not living by the sword applied to *all* Christians, it would have included this centurion. Thus, to reconcile self-defense-rejection with this story, the only way one can interpret Jesus' praise of the centurion is that Jesus condemns individual self-defense but not national self-defense. In other words, Christians can kill foreign enemies but not domestic enemies. Such an interpretation is absurd for many reasons. One cannot have it both ways: that Jesus condemns self-defense for individuals but not for the nation. If Jesus approves national defense, he approves individual self-defense because they rest on the same foundation.

That Jesus supported self-defense is shown further considering he paid (through monies found in a fish' mouth) taxes that "were applied to the soldier's wages, thus contributing to the support of the Roman army."[236] John the Baptist (the greatest man who ever lived and prepared the way of the Lord[237]) advanced the same idea when he instructed the publicans to "exact no more than that which is appointed,"[238] implying that taxes have legitimate purpose to support the government when the taxes are rightly assessed and not used to unjustly hurt others.

Similar to Jesus' approbation of the Roman centurion, John the Baptist answered a significant question from soldiers who asked about their duties in light of John's repent-and-be-baptized message. John the Baptist said, "Do violence to no man, neither accuse any falsely; and be content with your wages."[239] Doing violence to no man meant that the soldiers must not do violence unless good cause existed, which is based upon the natural principle of defending self and the nation. John's answer reflected Old Testament law and contained the following principles.

(1) harming man must be just;

(2) people have the right to defend themselves against criminal, tyrants, and foreign enemies;

(3) soldiers are equally bound by the natural law of doing no harm without just cause, as individuals are; and

(4) being a soldier is not about making money, but about protecting people.

John said a mouthful because his statement necessarily supported the right of self-defense for both individual and nation. So did Jesus.

Roman and Hebrew Self-Defense Philosophy Reconfirmed

In John's conversation with the Roman soldiers, he made no mention that soldiers should give up their swords and quit their duty. Rather, John accepted the *just war* doctrine and law of self-defense.[240] In truth, Roman law mirrored well-established Jewish law on the subject of self-defense and national defense.[241] As has been observed by historians, "Jewish law from the Bible was consistent with Roman law."[242] So, when John approved of the soldier's right to defend the nation for just cause, John accepted the same philosophy concerning the individual's right to defend himself for just cause.

Cicero wrote a few years prior to Jesus' birth and showed the Roman view of self-defense as follows.

What is the meaning of our retinues, what of our swords? Surely it would never be permitted to us to have them if we might never use them. This, therefore, is a law, O judges, not written, but born with us--which we have not learned, or received by tradition, or read, but which we have taken and sucked in and imbibed from nature herself; a law which we were not taught, but to which we were made--which we were not trained in, but which is ingrained in us--namely, that if our life be in danger from plots, or from open violence, or from the weapons of robbers or enemies, every means of securing our safety is honorable. For laws are silent when arms are raised, and do not expect themselves to be waited for, when he who waits will have to suffer an undeserved penalty before he can exact a merited punishment.[243]

In short, Roman and Hebrew philosophy said, "Self-Defense is established previous to all Laws".[244]

This philosophy recognized that the State is comprised of individuals and those individuals must protect themselves *individually* for the State to protect itself *collectively*. "The community...is one body made up of its individual members, and the community may act to 'defend the parts of its own body.'"[245] Romans thus viewed the individual's right to keep and bear arms equally important to the soldier's right.

They realized that where the people lose this right, the military's ability to protect the nation becomes impossible because of the impracticalities of protecting a defenseless nation. This reality has been described as follows.

The right to arms was abolished in 361 [A.D.], at least for persons who did not have advance approval from the government. However, the Empires' inability to protect their subjects led to a restoration of the right in 440 in both the Western and the Eastern Empires. The restoration was re-confirmed several years later by the Western Emperor Majorian Augustus.[246]

Clearly, where a nation is attacked by foreign enemies because the citizens are known to be effectively disarmed, the military's inability to fill that gap results in tragedy to that nation. The Romans and Hebrews therefore were expected to be armed so the nation could be fully protected.[247] American jurisprudence expressly continued this expectation and declared its vital important to securing a free State.[248] John's instruction to the Roman soldiers also showed this expectation.

The Roman philosophy that existed when Jesus lived developed more fully after his death, from Augustine of Hippo (354 A.D. – 430 A.D.) and expanding throughout Western Civilization. Notably, where the Jews fled because of persecution is where the right of self-defense dominated the legal, social, and political culture.[249] Undeniably, this philosophy formed the basis of American jurisprudence.[250] This accepted philosophy is noticeable given Jesus did not instruct his disciples on how and when to use the sword. The use of a sword is based upon what natural law and the Old Testament teaches concerning self-defense. Simon Peter recognized it when he was faced with it, and Jesus confirmed Peter was right when he described his ability to summon angels to defend them.

More than the right of self-defense against criminals, Roman philosophy recognized the people's right to resist public tyranny, much the way the Jewish people resisted King Saul when he intended to kill Jonathon for eating food. Individual and government oppressors were viewed similarly.

> A petty thief was no different in principle from a tyrant who stole the resources of his nation, or a nation which plundered another nation. The great Christian theologian, Augustine of Hippo, made a similar point, asking: "[If justice be taken away] . . . what are [governments] but [great bands of robbers]?"[251]

Consequently, Roman "soldiers [were]...subject to the ordinary law applicable to everyone else",[252] and "Roman law's rule [provided] that 'at night it is permissible to oppose a soldier who is breaking in, just as you would resist any other person, since no respect needs to be shown a soldier who has to be opposed with a weapon, as if he were a robber.'"[253]

In order of priority, the right of individual self-defense was first and the right of national defense was an extension of that right. So Roman philosophy held: the right of "reprisals [i.e. war] *originated in the same laws that governed self-defense*, the law of nations and divine law."[254] Therefore, John's approval of the soldier's right and duty to defend the nation is no small statement. He proclaimed the philosophy long held by Hebrews and Romans regarding self-defense and instructed these soldiers to follow it.

Argument 3: "Do Not Resist Evil"

One of the more significant arguments self-defense rejecters use to justify their position is Jesus' "resist not evil" statement in his Sermon on the Mount. Self-defense rejecters paint the Sermon on the Mount as philosophically different from the Old Testament. But in truth, "it contains many of the principles which Jesus articulated in the Sermon on the Mount, such as being kind to enemies or strangers."[255] Indeed, Jesus confirmed the Old Testament laws in all regards and accused the Pharisees for failing to (rightly) apply them.[256] Jesus' confirmation of the Old Testament included self-defense.

<u>Jesus Shows When Killing is Justified</u>

In his Sermon on the Mount, Jesus taught when killing is justified. As such, all of his other teachings do not contradict his teaching of what lawful killing is. He said,

> Ye have heard that it was said by them of old time, *Thou shalt not kill*; and whosoever shall kill shall be in danger of the judgment: But I say unto you, That whosoever is angry with his brother *without a cause* shall be in danger of the judgment.[257]

What Jesus said about anger shows what Jesus said about killing because he directly compared the *act* of killing to the *thought* of anger. Jesus said that whoever is angry with his brother *without cause* shall be in danger of the judgment. Jesus restated this Old Testament principle of "cause"[258] and described wrongful anger by

91

using the Old Testament term, "without [just] cause". When killing is without cause, it is unlawful, but when killing is with just cause, it is lawful.

Additionally, Jesus referred to and did not contradict one of the Ten Commandments, "thou shalt not kill". As such, Jesus invoked its Old Testament meaning and showed how the principle of "cause" applies to the heart *as well as* the body. Put differently, Jesus did not shrink Old Testament concepts; he expanded them. There is no doubt that "thou shalt not kill" did not mean a person could not kill another person when just cause existed. Killing was not only justified under the law but required depending on the circumstances. "[T]he law which God gave to the Israelites required use of deadly force in self-defense and defense of others."[259] So when Jesus uses this Old Testament concept to explain a New Testament concept, it shows that both are true. The following section is a further discussion on how Jesus used the Old Testament as the basis for New Testament teaching.

Jesus Uses Old Testament to Illustrate Christian Doctrine

Among Jesus' teachings in his Sermon on the Mount, he included concepts like, turn the other cheek, eye for eye, and love your enemies. Jesus used specific Old Testament concepts and invokes their meaning to explain Christian doctrine. In so doing, Jesus did not rid Christians of self-defense. Jesus upheld self-defense.

Turn the Other Cheek

Jesus said, "ye resist not evil: but whosoever shall smite thee on thy right cheek, turn to him the other also." Looking at the principles[260] of Jesus' teaching, it is not coincidence that he used the Old Testament concept, "turn the other cheek". As the Old Testament shows, turning the other cheek has its limits; and the specific reference to this teaching is found in Lamentations 3:30 (kjv), which states, "He giveth his cheek to him that smiteth him: he is filled full with reproach". Jesus' teaching mirrored this Old Testament version, and thus, the concepts are identical.

As Lamentations 3:31 (kjv) shows the Lord's impatience towards injustice ("the Lord will not cast off for ever"), Jesus showed that God does not approve of oppressors who deprive others of their rights. Jesus explained this, saying, "Blessed are the meek: for they shall inherit the earth."[261] Despite the misapplication of what it means to be meek, meekness does not mean, lie down and die. A person who is meek is one who does not oppress others but protects the oppressed. This is a universal principle for all: "The heaven, even the heavens, are the LORD'S: but the *earth hath he given to the children of men*."[262] God did not give the earth to man for the innocent to be oppressed. Rather, the "meek are those who...*follow [God's] directions*, and *comply with his designs*" for men on earth.[263] God's *direction and design* of preservation and protection were already defined in His law when Jesus arrived, and Jesus did not destroy that meaning.

Jesus furthered this same Old Testament truth concerning the meek, saying, the meek *shall* "inherit the earth". This is plainly a promise of earthly significance taken directly from Psalm 37:11 (kjv), which says, "the meek shall inherit the earth; and shall delight themselves in the abundance of peace." See the Old and New Testament connection between meekness and peace. Peace is the inheritance for those who seek it; and it is only obtained through principles of preservation and protection, enforced by peace seekers.[264] Consequently, though the "wicked watcheth the righteous, and seeketh to slay him",[265] the "LORD will not leave him [the meek] in his [the wicked's] hand, nor condemn him [the meek] when he is judged."[266] Significantly, Jesus' citation of this promise is "almost the only express temporal promise in all the New Testament",[267] and he chose the promise that supplies the defense of the poor, needy and upright.

In contrast to the meek inheriting the earth, oppressors inherit death. This is revealed in the book of Job.

> This is the portion of a wicked man with God, and the heritage of oppressors, which they shall receive of the Almighty. If his children be multiplied, it is for the sword: and his offspring shall not be satisfied with bread. Those that remain of him shall be buried in death: and his widows shall not weep.[268]

Even their wives do not weep when they are put to death and "[m]en shall clap their hands at him, and shall hiss him out of his place."[269] Their death justifiably comes from the meek that seek peace and accordingly protect innocent life. This was King David's prayer as well: "When he shall be judged, let him be condemned: and let his prayer become sin."[270]

God's uses people, and not just through government, to condemn oppression. This is significantly demonstrated in Moses when he defended the Hebrew slave being beaten by an Egyptian taskmaster. Moses' defense was no small task considering the source of the oppression.[271] Moses also used force to defend the Midian daughters who were being oppressed by evil shepherds. Moses "stood up"[272] against the shepherds and "helped" the daughters.[273] Clearly, Moses was a man of courage and despised injustice. Self-defense rejecters may attempt to undermine this Old Testament event; however, the New Testament explicitly praises Moses for his defense, showing the Christian principle of defending the innocent. Acts 7:24 (kjv) says, "seeing one of them suffer *wrong, he defended him*, and avenged him that was oppressed, and smote the Egyptian". Unfortunately, "[the Israelites] understood not" and continued to suffer wrong (i.e. against right) as a result. Similarly, self-defense rejecters understand not the justness of defending the innocent and spread a philosophical disease causing destruction and slavery. As was the case for Moses and is the case for any just man,[274] when the oppression increases, so increases the chances of resistance.[275]

Had Moses not been successful in his defense of Israel, his act would have been no less honorable. The Old and New Testament show that evil men have "condemned and killed the just",[276] for what practical power do (unarmed) people have against unlimited and arbitrary government force?[277] Regardless of pragmatics, however, the inevitable and rightful result of unjust killing is that man will defend his right to live in peace, whether through rebellion (as in the case of Moses), war (as in the case of Abraham[278]) or redress (as in the case of Esther[279])—"lest the people be ensnared".[280] As Psalm 37:14-15 (kjv) shows, this retribution comes by the sword.[281]

Like Abram who rescued Lot, God saw Moses as a leader to defend the defenseless and establish a free nation for God's people. But Moses would not have been this leader had he not "went out unto his brethren, and looked on their burdens."[282] Only judgment-blind people ignore oppression and choose to do nothing about it. Moses was not alone in his defense of the Hebrew children because God Himself ensured that the Israelites left Egypt *armed* with swords.[283] Significantly revealed, God's delivery of Israel began with Moses' use of the sword and ended with the people's possession of swords. Given "the majority of [New Testament] writers...praise [of] Moses"[284] and his appearance with Jesus in the disciples' presence,[285] Moses' exclaimed righteousness necessarily includes his act in defending the oppressed.

Self-defense rejecters refuse or fail to recognize the universal application that God created in the law of self-defense and foolishly attempt to turn Jesus against this law.

> Our Savior's words about giving to him that asketh, and turning the cheek to the smiter (Mat.5:39-42) must be interpreted by the principle of love that lies at the foundation of the law. Giving to every tramp and yielding to every marauder is not pleasing our neighbor "for that which is good unto edifying" (Rom. 15:2). Only by confounding the divine law with Scripture prohibition could one write..."Sin is the transgression of a divine law; but there is no divine law against suicide; therefore suicide is not sin."[286]

Self-defense rejecters refuse to admit that destroying God's universal law of self-defense only harms our neighbors and violates the universal law of love.

Showing further the significance of Jesus' using the Old Testament concept, consider how the book of Lamentations follows "turn the other cheek" by asserting the rights of man.

> For [the Lord] doth not afflict willingly nor grieve the children of men. To crush under his feet all the prisoners of the earth, *To turn aside the right of a man* before the face of the most High, To subvert a man in his *cause*, the *Lord approveth not.*[287]

This "cause of man"[288] is the same right Abraham used to convince God not to kill the innocent with the guilty.[289] It is the same right Moses considered when defending the Hebrew slave. It is the same right the righteous use to defend the innocent. It is the same right courts use when imposing punishment upon the guilty. It is the same right Christians used to form free societies and remove oppression from the people.

The book of Lamentations says, anyone who claims God approves of oppressing the innocent, denying the rights of others, and crushing the weak *distorts the views of God*. Therefore, Jesus "does not repeal the law of self-preservation, and the care we are to take of our families; we may avoid evil, and may resist it, so far as is necessary to our own security".[290] A patient man may accept a slap on the cheek, but he will moreover consider defending the rights of man.

Eye for Eye

Looking at Jesus' "eye for eye" statement, Jesus taught another Old Testament concept and highlighted the Pharisees' misuse of it. The Old Testament did not teach what the Pharisees were teaching. Rather, the law taught the following.

> If men strive, and hurt a woman with child, so that her fruit depart from her, and yet no mischief follow: he shall be surely punished, according as the woman's husband will lay upon him; and he shall pay as the judges determine. And if any mischief follow, then thou shalt give life for life, Eye for eye, tooth for tooth, hand for hand, foot for foot.[291]

This "eye for eye" law was given to Israel relative to (1) a person who hurts a pregnant woman resulting in her child's injury or death, and (2) the kind of punishment the judges must enact upon the finding of guilty in a criminal trial.

This law was to ensure that the judges were bound to execute equal punishment, that no favoritism would work against the poor, and that the value of the child's life would be protected. The same law and its purpose applied to other criminal acts as well.[292] In each case, the "eye for eye" law took place in a criminal trial and the statutory requirement of imposing sentence upon the guilty.

This requirement was a law of proportionality relative to criminal sentencing. This is the same standard God expressed in response to Cain killing Abel. "Whoso sheddeth man's blood, by man shall his blood be shed: for in the image of God made he man."[293]

> It was a direction to the judges of the Jewish nation what punishment to inflict in case of maims, for terror to such as would do mischief on the one hand, and for a restraint to such as have mischief done to them on the other hand, that they may not insist on a greater punishment than is proper: it is not a life for an eye, nor a limb for a tooth, but observe a proportion.[294]

This law was not a command that each person "render evil for evil" against fellow citizens, so that people would go about enforcing their own justice against all who "harmed" them.

The Pharisees were undermining this law's purpose and imposing their own agenda on the people. Jesus publically corrected their error and quickly received their resentment. As in virtually every other instruction, Jesus invoked the Old Testament in his Sermon on the Mount, explained its true meaning, and *broadened the concepts* of love to ensure the Pharisees were not abusing the people and the people knew the true sense of the law. This is a far cry from ridding Christians of preservation and protection.

Love Thy Enemy

Jesus proclaimed another Old Testament teaching in his sermon and again corrected what the Pharisees were teaching the Jews. He said,

> Ye have heard that it hath been said, Thou shalt love thy neighbour, and hate thine enemy. But I say unto you, Love your enemies, bless them that curse you, do good to them that hate you, and pray for them which despitefully use you, and persecute you.[295]

The Old Testament taught man to love his enemy too. This love is towards all man and causes him to treat them fairly and equitably.[296] Using the Old Testament as his source of definition, Jesus did not command passivism for Christians.[297] Walking an extra mile, giving one's coat, and such are inconveniences and were essential to the Old Testament law of love; but they are not close to having one's throat cut or arms severed and laying down to be "trodden under the foot of men".[298] The Old Testament did not teach that, nor did Jesus.

What is notable is how Jesus described "love thy enemy" compared to how he and the Apostles describe "love thy neighbor". In every instance where "love thy neighbor" is mentioned, it is always followed by "as thyself".[299] But where "love thy enemy" is mentioned, it is not qualified with "as thyself". This is significant because *loving thyself* is the most identifiable and fundamental form of love in the world. It relates to the two great earthly blessings of God at creation, *preservation and protection.* Self-love further serves as the universal method of identifying with other people. If one does not love himself, he cannot love or relate to others. When one hates himself, he is only a harm and detriment to society.

By using the qualifier, "as thyself," when describing loving one's neighbor and not using it when describing loving one's enemy, there is a clear difference between the two categories of love. Loving one's neighbor involves preserving and protecting. Loving one's enemy involves doing good to them, praying for their blessing, and not seeking their harm, which is what the Old Testament required of Israel too. As such, Jesus compared loving one's enemy to God's providing the sun and rain to the just and unjust alike.[300] That is, doing good to man generally is the mark of a peaceful and just man. However, loving one's enemy is limited by the greater obligation towards one's neighbors. God provides the sun and rain for the unjust and just alike, but God also punishes specific acts of evil and protects and avenges the innocent accordingly.

Applying this principle of love further, one cannot categorize Jesus sacrifice as the same as man's sacrifice. It is erroneous to say, since Jesus gave of himself voluntarily without any resistance, Christians must do the same. Jesus was God in flesh with all divine attributes, and as such, his sacrifice "conquered death, hell and the grave".[301] His death protected life. This was Jesus' power, and only he possessed it. Since man has no such divine power and since Jesus' sacrifice was once and for all,[302] man's sacrifice is earthly and relates to the power God put in man: preserving and protecting. By definition, a Christian's laying down his life for the brethren must be for the purpose of saving the lives of others,[303] just as Jesus death was intended to save man.

In summary, loving one's enemy does not mean allowing the enemy to kill you and your family, no more than loving your child requires you to let the child harm himself.

Jesus Responds to Specific Cultural Conditions

In addition to the analysis above, Jesus sermon was a response to specific cultural ills of his day. Jesus said in his sermon, "*you have heard it said*, An eye for an eye, and a tooth for a tooth". To begin his sermon, Jesus qualified his teaching to people who were hearing certain things from their religious leaders.[304] Given how Jesus treated the Pharisees throughout his ministry, Jesus had a major problem with their application of Jewish law, which he revealed more directly later. Jesus thus highlighted the difference between what the people were hearing and what God actually meant.[305] Clearly, Jesus intended to teach the people that correctly interpreting Scriptures is important and relying on what religious leaders say can distort true meaning. In doing this, Jesus confirmed what the Old Testament taught and clarified its misapplication by the Pharisees.

Violating the purpose of the law (i.e. eye for eye, tooth for tooth), the Pharisees enacted their own version of justice. They applied their own law and tradition to against people they found "deserving" of punishment.[306] Matthew Henry commented about these Pharisees.

> But some of the Jewish teachers, who were not the most compassionate men in the world, insisted upon it as necessary that such revenge should be taken, even by private persons themselves, and that there was no room left for remission, or the acceptance of satisfaction. Even now, when they were under the government of the Roman magistrates, and consequently the judicial law fell to the ground of course, yet they were still zealous for any thing that looked harsh and severe.

So, when Jesus stated, "Ye have heard that it hath been said", he did not attack Jewish law at all.[307] Rather, he was accusing the Pharisees for their harsh treatment of others in society *contrary to Jewish law*.

Jesus put the public on notice that they were being treated wrongfully by their own leaders and instructed the Pharisees not to ignore the greater matters of "judgment" (i.e. justice).[308] Jesus warned the people like this on other occasions as well, saying, "beware of the leaven of the Pharisees, and of the leaven of Herod."[309] Jesus' teachings did not create a new doctrine contrary to the law. He confirmed the importance of correctly following the moral laws of the Old Testament.

Argument 4: "Do Not Render Evil for Evil"

Self-defense rejecters also use the "render not evil for evil" verses to justify their position, but this has nothing to do with self-defense. "Render not evil for evil" teaches that people should not seek vengeance against those who have done them minor harm or inconvenience but should foster goodwill in society. This goodwill is advanced by letting personal inconveniences or trifles go, and where remedy is needed, using the proper "wrath" of government to repair civil wrongs. This avoids anarchy. Where government undermines or destroys the essence of protecting life, however, it steps outside of this teaching and requires a different response. This avoids tyranny. The element that remains in all cases is self-defense. Otherwise, anarchy or tyranny will result. To rid self-defense and to preserve evil is ludicrous.

The following verses are the New Testament verses describing the "render not evil for evil" teaching: 1 Thessalonians 5:15, 1 Peter 3:9, and Romans 12:17, each of which are addressed below. Before getting into the discussion, the definitions of the words should be shown. The word "render" (apodidōmi, G591) means "to pay back", and the word "evil" (kakos, G2556) means "worthless" or "wicked". In all three verses discussed below, the same words are used to instruct one of "render not evil for evil". As will be shown, self-defense cannot be "evil" and mean "paying back" an evil.

1 Thessalonians chapter 5

1 Thessalonians 5:15 (kjv) states, "[s]ee that none render evil for evil unto any man; but ever follow that which is good, both among yourselves, and to all men." The application of this instruction was to all people, not just Christians ("none", "any man", and "all men"). This universal application is similar to Paul's exhortation in Romans chapter 13 ("let *every soul* be subject") regarding submission to government. "Rendering not evil for evil" echoes the same principle that man should pursue social peace and avoid "fulfill[ing] the lusts [of the flesh]" to the harm of others.[310] These are lessons in civics as much as anything else and are not doctrines of slave-promotion.

Lawless justice creates chaos, perpetuates evil actions one against another,[311] and causes "souls to be spoiled".[312] At the core of God's instructions concerning all civil relationships,[313] promoting good and punishing evil is essential.[314] Just as man would not surrender everything he owns to a slothful neighbor, a man would not surrender all his rights to a tyrannous government.[315] The balance of civil life must be sought by Christians, which requires one to understand how to avoid the two extremes of anarchy and tyranny. At the center of this is self-defense.

Deuteronomy 24:10 (kjv) shows how anarchy is avoided by having just laws to govern man's civil relationships. It states, "When thou dost lend thy brother any thing, thou shalt not go into his house to fetch his pledge." Self-help remedies undermine harmonious society and lawful government. Romans 12:19 (kjv) explains this same principle and shows what man should do instead of exercising self-help. "[A]venge not yourselves, but rather give place unto wrath". The "wrath" man should seek prefers the wrath of government (described in Romans 13:4) over self-help because government provides a neutral method and common authority for resolving civil disputes. Simply stated, rendering evil for evil is where a person tries to enforce his own civil remedies in society when government is available to resolve the civil dispute neutrally and fairly. This, however, assumes that government and law actually protect the rights of the person not at fault.[316] When that no longer happens, different problems arise and must be remedied.

Underlying Paul's lesson in civics is this: where government and law destroy rights, self-help may be used to save the greater (man) at the expense of the lesser (government/law). The point of when self-help is used is a matter conscience and social response. There is no exact formula for every society, but the American Declaration of Independence expressed the philosophy this way.

> [M]ankind are more disposed to suffer, while evils are sufferable, than to right themselves by abolishing the forms to which they are

accustomed. But when a long train of abuses and usurpations, pursuing invariably the same Object evinces a design to reduce them under absolute Despotism, it is their right, it is their duty, to throw off such Government, and to provide new Guards for their future security.[317]

America's Declaration of Independence shows that at some point the people must resist government to accomplish the greater good for man. In other words, the greater evil of death and destruction caused by government must be stopped by the people so that better government can protect the people's life and rights.

On the opposite side of anarchy is tyranny, and it produces similar evils. Just as anarchy is to be avoided by not rendering evil for evil, tyranny is to be avoided by preventing oppression of the innocent. This is why Paul follows his discussion rebuking anarchy in Romans chapter 12 with the purpose of government in Romans chapter 13. As a matter of additional historical observation, Paul's discussion on the subject is the description of "liberty" given by the father of the United States Constitution, James Madison.

Happily for mankind, *liberty* is not…confined to any single point of time; but *lies within extremes*, which afford sufficient latitude for all the variations which may be required by the various situations and circumstances of civil society.[318]

People thus institute government to avoid the two extremes, and Paul demonstrates this in the book of Romans.

Nowhere does Scriptures describe self-defense as an evil. Just the opposite: it is defined as good. It is, in fact, the only way to avoid social chaos and establish peace in society. To render "evil" towards another person necessarily excludes self-defense, and "to him that knoweth to do good, and doeth it not, to him it is sin."[319] Were self-defense to be included in the "render not evil for evil" meaning, the verse would read "render not good or evil for an evil". The opposite is instructed throughout Scriptures: overcome evil with good.

<u>1 Peter chapter 3</u>

1 Peter chapter 3 adds further light on the subject of "not rendering evil for evil". It says in verses 8 through 11,

> Finally, be ye all of one mind, having compassion one of another, love as brethren, be pitiful, be courteous: Not rendering evil for evil, or railing for railing: but contrariwise blessing; knowing that ye are thereunto called, that ye should inherit a blessing. For he that will love life, and see good days, let him refrain his tongue from evil, and his lips that they speak no guile: Let him eschew evil, and do good; let him seek peace, and ensue it.

In addition to the analysis above, God commands us in 1 Peter 3:8 to have *compassion* one of another, meaning "having a fellow feeling" (G4841).

Compassion comes from recognizing in others the like attributes of human nature.[320] "[W]e must have a tender concern for all that share with us in the human nature, and as we have opportunity; (that is, according to their necessities and our abilities) we must do good to all men".[321] Compassion is the natural sentiment we *should* feel about man in general but certainly our family and friends. There is no greater natural sentiment in man than this: that life is a gift[322] and deserving of protection. Those who recognize this act accordingly. Those who do not recognize this defy God's creation[323] and reject the "principles of Jesus".[324] They act accordingly as well by not preserving or protecting life. Malachi 2:10 (kjv) states this duty man has towards others. "Have we not *all one father*? hath not *one God created us*? why do we deal treacherously every man against his brother?"[325] Dealing treacherously with others includes ignoring the duty to defend innocent life. This duty is the foundation of forming government: to bear the sword not in vain but for the purpose of punishing evil and promoting good.[326]

More than government bearing the sword, Proverbs 24:10-12 (kjv) describes our duty to defend innocent people "drawn to death" and "ready to be slain" unjustly as follows.

> If thou faint in the day of adversity, thy strength is small. If thou forbear to deliver them that are drawn unto death, and those that are ready to be slain; If thou sayest, Behold, we knew it not; doth not he that pondereth the heart consider it? and he that keepeth thy soul, doth not he know it? and shall not he render to every man according to his works.

In light of this duty, Job proclaimed the appropriate judgment on those, including himself, who shirk this duty to defend the innocent. He said, "let mine arm fall from my shoulder blade, and mine arm be broken from the bone."[327] In other words, if one does not help fellow man, especially those who need it most, then he should not be equipped with those body members that enable his preservation and protection. King David likewise said, "If I have rewarded evil unto him that was at peace with me...let him tread down my life upon the earth, and lay mine honour in the dust.[328]

1 Peter chapter 3 shows further its true sense by stating, "not rendering...*railing for railing*", which immediately follows the command "not rendering evil for evil". The word "railing" is a Greek word that means "slander", which is speaking evil against another person without cause. This verse teaches people not to cause unnecessary strife and discord through words. Titus 3:2 (kjv) puts it this way, "To speak evil of no man, to be no brawlers, but gentle, shewing all meekness unto all men". Is this a universal command, like self-defense rejecters claim of "not rendering evil for evil" (as well as "be ye subject unto the higher powers")?

Given Jesus' publically calling the Pharisees "vipers" and worse,[329] "not rendering railing for railing" shows that condemning others is not an absolute command. No, it does not proscribe Christians from condemning evil behavior when necessary, which to Jesus meant executing the weightier matter of justice.[330] Similarly, given Jesus' display of throwing the money changers out of the Temple,[331] not "brawling" with "all men" is not a universal command of pacifism. This same analysis is true regarding "render not evil for evil". Jesus showed that sometimes verbal accusation and physical brawling are necessary to comply with one's greater duties.

1 Peter chapter 3 further commands us to "love life and see good days" (verse 10). To do this, Christians must "eschew [shun] evil, and do good; let him seek peace, and ensue it" (verse 11).[332] To shun evil, do good and seek peace mean one must comply with his duties to man,[333] which includes protecting innocent life. Any contrary "oath" creates only harm and death to the innocent in perpetuity, which is sinful. Saying "peace, peace" and praying for peace amount to nothing where people ignore the duty to act and when that duty is within their power.[334] Seeking peace are *actions* that prevent evil people from taking advantage of others.[335]

Those who argue that peace is obtained through giving up arms and self-defense are diluted. This delusional view of Scriptures has been advanced as follows.

> Now should not all who are seeking to promote the present and eternal welfare of their fellow men, unite in one great and untiring effort to abolish, to banish from the earth this cruel, demoralizing and destructive scourge [of national defense]...Will not all Christians fully agree that war is a grievous violation of the principles of our holy religion?[336]

This version of "seeking peace" is totalitarian at best, and God forbid its worst. It presumes that not taking up arms accomplishes God's best on earth. It presumes that allowing people to be trodden under the feet of tyrants shows the love of God. Such a one equates not resisting evil to following God's commandments, stating, "What right have we to hope for eternal life, if knowingly and habitually we violate his commandments? 'If ye love me, keep my commandments.'"[337] These self-defense rejecters fail to consider any earthly duties towards man and distort what "keep my commandments" really means. Shamefully, they prefer that innocent people, including women and children, be the fodder for the wicked—all in the name of "following Christ".

Hypocritically, self-defense rejecters decry the right of individual, and perhaps even national, self-defense and yet do nothing to prevent people from acting in self-defense. If the question were put to them, do you think our laws should punish people for using self-defense? Their answer would likely be, no. This begs the question, why? Logic demands, if Christians have the *duty not to bear the sword*, then they should put God's command of civics into legal effect.

Revealing the absurdity of self-defense-rejection, self-defense rejecters (more than likely) support "pro-life" candidates because "our laws should protect innocent life". But how can they claim such a thing? If God rids the born of self-defense, he moreover rids the unborn of self-defense and all talk about enforcing God's moral laws is the epitome of hypocrisy. Alternatively, if laws should protect the unborn from unjust killing (which recognizes their right to live), it should preserve the right of self-defense (which also recognizes the right to live). How can self-defense rejecters claim otherwise? Getting to where the rubber meets the road, self-defense rejecters propose that the greater commandment of God is to be slaughtered, not to protect life. They do so even though the entire law of God opposes their position. Still, upon self-defense-rejection principles, no Christian should ever attempt to defend an innocent person, including unborn babies. Unknowingly or not, however, Christians in America violate their "scriptural rule" every day. Here is why.

Laws are only the collective power of the individual's natural right to use the sword for preservation and protection. Every judicial order that takes the life of a criminal uses the individual rights of that society to punish the convicted person. Similarly, every soldier who kills a person in battle kills under the same authority of individuals. Every Christian in America is included in those killings through our political constitutions. In truth, this is how God views criminal retribution, including the death penalty, as well (discussed further below).

If self-defense rejecters are to reconcile their "conviction" against abortion with their self-defense rejection, they have two logical choices:

> (1) stop trying to protect the unborn (through voting, donating or otherwise) and let those babies be killed because it is their God-imposed duty; or

(2) advocate for the revocation of all laws sanctioning self-defense and war because those laws and acts are performed through the power and consent of *We the People* (that includes you, self-defense rejecters).

If self-defense rejecters are not willing to do this, their faith is without works. The truth is, they cannot reconcile any attempt to preserve the good of humanity through law (domestically and internationally) with their doctrine. What is worse, self-defense rejecters do nothing to enforce what they claim God imposes. Their doctrine is rhetoric with no positive influence in life.

We should get back to reality. Who are we as fellow humans to deny the rights of the innocent for the sake of preserving the lusts of evil men?[338] The duty of preservation and protection is imposed upon all man including Christians, and complying with this duty is the work of righteousness.[339] Not complying with this duty is "contrary to nature".[340] A Christian has no "duty" to act in way that results in calamity to everyone around him, nor can a Christian claim that his "personal conviction" of passivism is made in isolation. Every decision to give up the right of self-defense poses harm to one's neighbors. "For none of us liveth to himself, and no man dieth to himself."[341] This is not a duty imposed by God. It is concocted by man.

Romans chapter 12

Romans chapter 12 further explains man's duties relative to "not rendering evil for evil". Romans 12:17

states, "Recompense to no man evil for evil. Provide things honest in the sight of all men." In addition to the analysis above, Romans 12:18 (kjv) reveals that it is not always possible to avoid violence with others (as Jesus shows[342]). It says, *"If it be possible*, as much as lieth in you, live peaceably with all men" (emphasis added). Clearly, times happen when protecting innocent life becomes one's duty. This duty has always been considered good by scriptural definition. So when Romans 12:21(kjv) states, "Be not overcome of evil, but overcome evil with good", self-defense is the good that may and should be used, when necessary, to overcome evil.

Significant to understanding "render not evil for evil", one must consider what Paul wrote in Romans chapters 12 and 13, as well as chapter 15.

- Romans chapter 12 teaches men to avoid anarchy and to seek peace in society.

- Romans chapter 13 teaches why we have government and should submit to it: to promote good and punish evil.

- Romans chapter 15 teaches how we should help our neighbors.

Leviticus 25:17 (kjv) summarizes their teachings, "Ye shall not therefore oppress one another".[343] This teaching formed the basis of free societies throughout history, including Israel. It includes more than the right of self-defense; it includes the rights of equal protection,[344] due process[345] and democracy.[346] In truth, this principle is universally accepted to maintain any free society and government. "It is for the sins of a people that God...hides from their eyes the things that belong to the public peace."[347]

Indeed, Israel was acquainted with the evil effects of being oppressed "every one by another, and *every one by his neighbor*",[348] but God desired that Israel live not in oppression but freedom. Self-defense is self-evidently essential to preventing oppression and maintaining peace in society; that is, to avoid both anarchy and tyranny.[349] Scriptures reveal, every person is bound by this social *oath*—that preservation and protection be maintained.[350] Any oath to the contrary is a nullity[351] and results in the earth being filled with violence.[352] No man can be bound by an oath to have his life taken without just cause, no more than an oath to kill oneself can be enforced. "He hath put forth his hands against such as be at peace with him: he hath *broken his covenant*", says Psalm 55:20 (kjv).[353] Breaking this universal covenant only shows one's distortion of Scriptures and God's universal design.[354]

The criminal laws in Israel were based upon this oath as well. When a person was criminally convicted and punished, the people imposed the punishment "as one man".[355] In other words, each citizen imposed the punishment upon the guilty but they did it collectively as a society.[356] They performed through corporate act because when one harmed another in society, the entire society was harmed by the criminal act.

The foundation for this oath and act is based on the reason society is formed and maintained: to protect each and all—to use collective will and force in defending and avenging rights and improving human condition. When one person is vulnerable to harm, then everyone is. If person "A" can be harmed without cause in such a fashion, then so could person "B" and every person in society *infinitum*. God thus required in Deuteronomy 17:7 (kjv), "The hands of the witnesses shall be first upon him to put him to death, and afterward the hands of all the people. So thou shalt put the evil away from among you."[357] Historians observe as well that Roman philosophy adopted the same oath and rule of law (which existed during Jesus' day), saying, "all forms of theft [are] as merely variations on a single type of attack on society."[358] Both Romans and Hebrews exercised their rights of preservation and protection upon those who violated this oath and ridded themselves of brutes in society who violated their oath to each and all.

Today's American Christians do the same as Israel because *We the People* possess the political power that creates death penalty laws for domestic defense and war for national defense. Thus, this question is begged again: if you believe God imposes a duty on Christians not to defend themselves, then what are you doing to change the laws in America to reflect that duty? If nothing, you have no standing to persuade others you are right. The reality is, no sane person would ever remove a law that protects them, their loved ones and neighbors. This means that such laws of protection *should* remain and implies that moral requirement of self-defense. This is further true because self-defense protects what is right and resists what is evil, just as Romans chapter 13 declares is the purpose for government.

In truth, the only way government can legitimately bear the sword to punish evil and protect good is because man (each and all) has the inherent right to defend himself.[359] Were God to destroy man's right of self-defense, government would have no basis to enforce justice in society on behalf of individuals. Governments that forsake this basic element of human existence are not ordained by God and have no authority to rob people of their original right of self-defense.[360] By helping to sustain our self-defense laws, self-defense rejecters implicitly agree with the truth of self-defense. Their position is made clearer by their actions than by their theology, and their words are as one fighting the air.[361] Their doctrine means nothing and has no practical effect in life.

CHAPTER 4

The Christian's Response

If a Christian has come to the conclusion that he has a right and duty to defend against criminals and tyrants, then he must learn what that means today. The philosophy of self-defense has been discussed for thousands of years. It boils down to this: "law imposes two basic requirements [in] self-defensive armed responses: *necessity* and *proportionality*."[362] Together, necessity and proportionality form the *lower* and *upper* limits of meaningful self-defense. These elements of self-defense (1) justify enough force to overcome the harm (necessity - lower limit) and (2) show how much force is necessary to overcome the harm (proportionality - upper limit).[363] When either element is undermined, self-defense loses its purpose and effect.

These elements apply to individuals and nations alike, and they are contained in the Constitution of the United States of America. Using them, along with the Second Amendment's meaning, the Christian will oppose attempts to remove the elements of necessity and proportionality. Specific to today's sociopolitical environment, the Christian should oppose attempts to criminalize and unreasonably regulate the citizens' right and power to own and use semi-automatic rifles. The elements of *necessity* and *proportionality* are discussed below.

Necessity

"The necessity requirement focuses on the *type and degree* of force [needed] to overcome the enemy".[364] The Second Amendment of the Constitution of the United States of America expresses what "necessity" means in a civil and political setting. It expresses that keeping and bearing arms possessed by citizens is *necessary* to secure a Free State from government tyranny—foreign and domestic. History shows, the Constitution intended "arms" to mean a weapon of war held by soldiers. That weapon was and still is a soldier's battle rifle. Without this weapon, the people would be deprived of the necessary tool of self-defense. So the Second Amendment guarantees the citizens' right to keep a battle rifle.

Opposing the laws of necessity, some in America today are trying to ever widen the gap between the government's weapons and capabilities and the people's personal self-defense weapon. They are trying to increase the government's power and eliminate the people's in this regard. This is dangerous to liberty, and the Second Amendment expresses the same when it says, "to secure a Free State". Regardless of time, "[the people must] view [government] with a spirit of jealous acquiescence in a necessary evil, and *stand ready to resist* a power which they suppose *may be exerted* to the prejudice of their rights".[365] Practicing what this teaches, the people must bear arms necessary to resist tyrants. In

1787 it meant a battle rifle, and it still means that today, except now it specifically means the semi-automatic rifle.

The reason semi-automatic rifles with sufficient magazine capacity are necessary, keeping with the Second Amendment's purpose, is because it is the only weapon of a personal nature similar to the soldier's weapon and capable of serving meaningful self-defense. No other weapon effectively serves this function. Revolvers, pistols and shotguns may be meaningful relative to resist most criminals, but they are inadequate to hinder the tyrant and a number of soldiers. Being mindful of Jesus' instructions to his disciples to buy a sword, one must remember that the sword Jesus spoke of was the same sword (the Roman sword) that the Apostle Paul said that government wielded ("He beareth not the sword in vain") to punish evil. Simply put, Jesus instructed his disciples to keep and bear a military-type defense arm. And in modern parlance, only the semi-automatic rifle fits this standard.

In summation, the citizen's semi-automatic rifle most completely serves the element of *necessity* in securing a Free State because of its ability to (1) directly target an enemy's imminent and proximate attack, (2) put sufficient distance between the enemy and the citizen, (3) increase the chances of meaningful defense or escape, and (4) deter the tyrant's willingness to use deadly force against the citizenry. Under this formula, tyrants "will be unable to enforce encroachments against the united efforts of the great body of the people."[366] But there is another element of self-defense that must be applied: proportionality.

Proportionality

"Proportionality can be determined by evaluating the (1) *magnitude of the risk* that a lawful self-defense action seeks to prevent (2) in the *context of its probability*".[367] While necessity addresses why personal self-defense are needed in the first place (i.e. to maintain a Free State), proportionality defines the relation between the potential for harm and the degree of response needed to prevent the harm. It has been said, "[p]roportionality…is intended to ensure a 'functional connection between the aims and the means of actions of self-redress'."[368] In other words, citizens must maintain weaponry that rises to a proportional functional level between the potential of domestic (and foreign) oppression and the citizens' capacity to successfully respond to that threat. Proportionality's elements of (1) magnitude of the risk and (2) context of its probability are discussed below.

Magnitude of Risk

The magnitude of the risk in a civil context essentially means two things: (1) losing liberty (and the State) through domestic oppression and (2) losing liberty (and the nation) through foreign oppression. Of the two, America's history shows that the people drafting and ratifying our Constitution were concerned about the first risk as much as the second. Americans were very skeptical about a standing military being used by the federal government against the people and States and feared their forceful power over a defenseless people. Thus, they did not leave liberty's and their States' protection to the better parts of man's nature. As James Madison said, "If men were angels, no government would be necessary. If angels were to govern men, neither external nor internal controls on government would be necessary."[369] Americans knew more than internal controls on government (i.e. checks and balances) are necessary to secure a free state. External controls are necessary (i.e. the people's power of self-defense).

Americans who ratified the Constitution insisted on guarantees of the people's rights, not just in a political sense, but in a practical sense. Among the most practical defense methods against despotism, the Second Amendment was the essence of this guarantee, and it had this explicit purpose: to allow the people to defend themselves with arms and prevent being governed *against their consent*. The magnitude of the risk of losing liberty was very specific and real because it derived from the force of a large, powerful and centralized government funded by the people (and perhaps foreign interests) and governed by men who have the potential of imposing evil upon others.

Alexander Hamilton described the magnitude of the risk as follows.

> [I]f the defense of the community...should make it necessary to have an army so numerous as to hazard its liberty, this is one of those calamaties

for which there is neither preventative nor cure. It cannot be provided against by any possible form of government.[370]

Despite suggestions to remedy this risk by limiting military power, Hamilton (and ultimately the Constitution) rejected the suggestion. Hamilton observed that a nation cannot be limited in protecting itself against foreign threat. The Constitution must not favor foreign invasion for the sake of reducing the risk of domestic oppression. Put simply, as the foreign threat against a nation increases, so must the nation's defense capacity. Still, in such a case, the potential threat to the people increases, so there must be a counter-balancing effect.

To counter-balance the growth of the military's power, the citizens' ability to protect themselves from despotic domestic government must also grow in proportion. To be clear, the *form of government* is not the citizens' ultimate protection. More than that, it is their ability to protect themselves with arms. Alexander Hamilton expressed this as follows.

> If the representatives of the people betray their constituents, there is then no resource left but in the exertion of that original right of self-defense...The obstacles to usurpation and the facilities of resistance increase with the increased extent of the state, provided the citizens understand their rights and are disposed to defend them."[371]

Considering the requirement of proportionality, Alexander Hamilton confirmed that the people's power *must increase* as the government's power increases and in addition, notes that the people must understand their rights and be willing to defend them. Hamilton further said on the subject,

> The natural strength of the people in a large community, *in proportion* to the artificial strength of the government, is greater than in a small, and of course more competent to a struggle with the attempts of the government to establish a tyranny.[372]

> For a long time to come, it will not be possible to maintain a large army; and as the means of doing this increase, the population and natural strength of the community will *proportionably increase*. [If the] time arrive[s] that the federal government can raise and maintain an army capable of erecting a despotism...the people...[will] take measures for their own defense.[373]

The people's power increases proportionally with the government's military power in these ways: (1) the number of people who know how to use arms proficiently, (2) the citizens keep personal weapons substantially similar to the military's personal weapons, and (3) the citizens being able to have a sufficient number of weapons and ammunition to defend against military force.

Some challenge the need of citizens having arms similar to soldiers' arms, but such a person ignores the philosophical and practical reasons for having like weapons. They argue, "It is insulting to say that citizens need military-type weapons to protect themselves against the military or police because our military will never turn against Americans." The argument is illogical at best, and our Constitution rejects the notion. If their argument is true, however, the question is begged, why does one give more credit to the military or police than to the citizenry?

Are the citizens to be trusted less than the military such that their means of proportional defense are *presumed* unnecessary? And more than unnecessary, proportional defense is made criminal! Are citizens so untrustworthy that the government must create a crime out of possessing a legitimate tool? Are we to assume citizens are dangerous and ill-intended but those in the military and police are not susceptible to following evil orders? America's founders did not think so, nor did they place undue trust in those who possess military and police power without leaving to the people the ability and right of defending themselves against potential threats. The essence of the Constitution is based on the truth that all humans and governments are capable of oppressing others, not just criminals but government.

Given that the citizenry will not be trained and organized in military tactics, strategy and practice, the people have only two main benefits over the military: (1) a high population and (2) similar personal weaponry that can be used proficiently. Alexander Hamilton illustrated this well as follows.

> [I]f circumstances should at any time oblige the government to form an army of any magnitude

that army can never be formidable to the liberties of the people while there is a large body of citizens, little, if at all, inferior to them in discipline and the use of arms, who stand ready to defend their own rights and those of their fellow-citizens. This appears to me the only substitute that can be devised for a standing army, and the best possible security against it, if it should exist.[374]

If it is true that nations will proportionally increase their military depending on another nation's military growth,[375] the same is true internally relative to the citizenry, which is a militia force of their own right.[376] It is foolish to decrease the citizens' means of self-defense as the government continually grows.

Directly opposed to what some are attempting, America's foundation rests on the knowledge that the people will be proportionally capable of resisting attempted despotism.[377] "[S]uppose the national rulers actuated by the most ungovernable ambition[;] it is impossible to believe that they would employ such preposterous means to accomplish their designs" *when the people are proportionally armed.*[378] Were this foundation removed, there would be little, if not nothing, to discourage or prevent despots from using brute force to impose their will on the people.

Context of Probability

Context of probability means this: under what circumstances would the citizens' self-defense be likely necessary and what kind of force would be necessary to respond. America's history reveals the context of probability, noting both human experience and nature. The *context of probability* involves the government's use of military against Americans—a military despotism—as has already been shown. "These armies being...called into activity for interior [offense], the people are in [] danger of being broken to military subordination."[379] Simply stated, where the military's force exists within the nation, the people are in danger of being oppressed by them. This hazard began and remains as a part of our Constitution's natural composition. But today, the context is much larger.

The federal government has increased the number of police agencies exponentially, so now this presents another "context of probability". Americans once saw very little of the federal government because its administration had mostly to do with international and interstate commercial concerns.[380] In his attempt to persuade the States to ratify the Constitution, Alexander Hamilton observed that the federal government would be at a natural disadvantage to oppress the people because the States, not the federal government, administer the civil and criminal justice systems. As such, the federal government would not have the kind of police power States do to unjustly arrest and prosecute the people. Today, this is no longer the case.

The federal government has created its own system of civil and criminal laws that are as extensive, if not more, than the States' police power, but without the close connection the State officials have to the people.

This means that as the federal government passes laws and enforces them, the federal government will have a significant potential for power abuse. This is true because of the distance between federal officials and local communities. It is not an unreasonable argument to make that the federal government is practically unaccountable to the people based upon the laws of proportionality and relativity. This means that the further away the people are to the government and the greater the numbers of people are in relation to the government, the less accountable the government is to the people.

Given this upside-down happening over the years, the *context of probability* has expanded. Now, federal despotism against the people can come in a myriad of ways and through a variety of sources. This is not to say that the increase of government police power may not rightly take place in society based upon needs and circumstances. However, just as when the military grows, the people's power must increase; the same is true relative to government police power. Given this truth, the people must be proportionally armed to resist any potential government threat against them, whether military or police.

This maxim is more applicable and relevant given how politicians have been attempting to rob Americans of the right to keep the kind of arms that are necessary and proportional to secure a Free State. What should be happening instead is, the people's ability to keep arms should be increasing. If it is necessary that the people be proportionally armed to secure a Free State, it follows that where the people are disproportionally armed, the people will not be able to secure a Free State. There is only one reason this can become reality, and Alexander Hamilton expressed it as follows.

> [The people must] *stand ready to defend their own rights and those of their fellow-citizens.* This appears to me *the only substitute* that can be devised for a standing army, and the *best possible security* against it, if it should exist.[381]

It should be obvious that Jesus' command to his disciples to obtain a combat-effective Roman sword (the same kind that Roman soldiers bore) was his approbation for the principle of proportionality. Reason, Scriptures, and experience all prove why proportionality is required. Christians only harm themselves and others by not ensuring this critical element of self-defense remains intact in America.

CONCLUSION

Self-defense rejecters hold an absurd position. Their doctrine is self-conflicting, contradictory ideas that can never be reconciled in the real world God created for all humanity. They hold a theory as erroneous as "Scriptures prove the world is flat". They fail to acknowledge that God created duties and powers as well as rights and responsibilities that should not be surrendered by any generation or dispensation. Their doctrine is brutish and serves only to encourage evil doers to take advantage of ignorant Christians. It serves to perpetually incite foreign enemies to ransack our nation endlessly and enable our government to more easily oppress the people. Their burden of proof is high, and they fail to come close to the threshold of persuasion.

Christians can be assured that God kept intact the universal right of self-defense and that they have a right to use it when the circumstances require. Christians have a duty to protect their own household, community and nation. Christians have an obligation to ensure society lives in an environment of preservation and protection. When one realizes the scriptural support for self-defense, he will see the importance self-defense plays in preserving liberty and freedom for America's generations. The right of self-defense existed prior to all laws, and the Second Amendment secures this right so

Americans could protect themselves against criminal and tyrant. Yet, it is under attack on many levels.

Knowing this, Christians must think and act in ways that protect the *necessity* and *proportionality* of self-defense. Christians must realize that the government's turning the means of self-defense into a "hall pass" of permission destroys the two elements of self-defense and that turning gun possession into government privilege undermines what it means to be a citizen of a Free State—one who stands ready and willing to protect individuals of society from foreign and domestic enemies.

Some will stop at nothing to rid America of its philosophical and constitutional foundations and to eliminate practical political power of individuals and place it in the hands of bureaucrats and elitists. That agenda is clear and real. Sadly, they have gained a lot of ground. Equally sad, many Christians have failed to see the significance of the Second Amendment's purpose and have shied away too often at the confrontation. This must stop.

The future of liberty and constitutional government in America rests on what we as Americans and Christians are thinking and doing today. Government and laws—the ordinance of God—is a monumental business to be engaged and occupied by children of God. There is no excuse for Christians' indifference in the area of social and political liberty. Nor is there excuse for church goers to support pastors that teach a fallacious doctrine that promotes slavery to men. At the top of this consideration is the right of meaningful defense.

There may come a day when imbecilic politicians are able to successfully enact laws that rob Americans of rights we have enjoyed for centuries. That such a thing could happen should cause Christians to muster the courage demonstrated by our Christian forefathers, like Abraham and Moses, whose calling from God rested on their acts of defense. Christians should fortify their dedication not to let evil people fracture America by insisting that we give up liberty and rights because of their unreasonable and maniacal agenda. Christians should not permit these people to force dismay throughout the United States by turning fundamental right into government oversight. What Christians do in response during these days is crucial to the future success of America as a free nation.

If Christians do not become convicted about the most fundamental matter of our existence as God's creation, then perhaps nothing will. But if Christians see the need for protecting and preserving life against criminal and tyrant, they will also see the importance in not surrendering their right to self-defense and thus, their guns, of which the semi-automatic rifle stands supreme.

ENDNOTES

[1] David B. Kopel, *The Human Right Of Self-Defense*, BYU Journal of Public Law, 22 BYUJPL 43 (2007), 43.

[2] Ibid. at 45.

[3] See, James chapter 2 (kjv).

[4] "For even when we were with you, this we commanded you, that if any would not work, neither should he eat." 2 Thessalonians 3:10 (kjv).

[5] "[I]f there is a set of universally applicable epistemological standards for the justification of factual truth claims, at least a prima facie case exists for applying those standards to the justification of positive propositions of law." Gary Lawson, *Proving The Law*, 86 NWULR 859 Northwestern University Law Review, (Summer, 1992), 865-866.

[6] That Natural Law confirms the right of self-defense is too self-evident to require explanation. In addition, this confirmation has been developed over thousands of years of philosophical history. It is also confirmed in the Old Testament expressly. Rightly noted, "[T]he right of self-defence is founded in nature and developed in natural law which is simply the law of the Creator, and is both unwritten and revealed." Snowden, George Randolph, *The Christian's Right to Bear Arms*, (Philadelphia, PA, 1911), 5. "[T]he most fundamental of all [natural rights is] the right of self-preservation". Brian Tierney, *The Idea of Natural Rights: Studies on Natural Rights, Natural Law and Church Law*, (Emory University, 1997) 70. "Moreover, one hardly needs to believe in natural law to recognize self-defense as a fundamental right. When we examine the sources of international law, we will not expect to find that all the great founders of international law were unanimous in their epistemology, or that all their sensibilities are congruent with our own. Wherever one thinks rights come from, it is quite

significant that there is unanimity of opinion among the founders of international law: personal self-defense is a fundamental human right, essential to the foundation of international law and order." Kopel, *The Human Right Of Self-Defense*, 101-102. "Under both the U.N. Charter and customary international law, self-defense is an 'inherent' right." Katherine M. Royal, *Burning The Barn To Roast The Pig? Proportionality Concerns In The War On Terror And The Damadola Incident,* Willamette Journal of International Law and Dispute Resolution (2006), 54-55.

[7] Pre-Mosaic: "And the Horites in their mount Seir, unto Elparan, which is by the wilderness...And they took Lot, Abram's brother's son, who dwelt in Sodom, and his goods, and departed...And when Abram heard that his brother was taken captive, he armed his trained servants, born in his own house, three hundred and eighteen, and pursued them unto Dan." Genesis 14:6,12,14 (kjv). Post-Mosaic: "If the thief is found breaking in, and he is struck so that he dies, there shall be no guilt for his bloodshed." Exodus 22:2 (kjv). See also, "all [rabbinic scholars] agreed with the core principle that self-defense is permissible in cases of necessity." David B. Kopel, *The Torah and Self-Defense*, Penn State Law Review, 109 PENNSTLR 17 (Summer 2004), 27.

[8] "Think not that I am come to destroy the law, or the prophets: I am not come to destroy, but to fulfil." Matthew 5:17 (kjv). "Christ commands nothing now which was forbidden either by the law of nature or the moral law, nor forbids any thing which those laws had enjoined; it is a great mistake to think he does, and he here takes care to rectify the mistake". Matthew Henry, *Commentaries on the Bible*, commenting on Matthew 5:17-20. See also, "For whatsoever things were written aforetime were written for our learning, that we through patience and comfort of the scriptures might have hope." Romans 15:4 (kjv); "Jesus Christ the same yesterday, and to day, and for ever." Hebrews 13:8 (kjv).

[9] Job 8:3 (kjv).

[10] Lawson, *Proving The Law*, 859.

[11] "Any person purporting to make a warranted truth claim of any sort, in the context of a legal discussion or otherwise, must be prepared to answer each of these questions: what did you count, or not count, as evidence of truth or falsity; how heavily did you count it; and how much evidence, and of what quality, did you require before making your claim?" Ibid. at 871.

[12] Ed. Bryan A. Garner, Black's Law Dictionary, 7th Ed. (West Group, St. Paul, MN, 2000).

[13] "A theory's determinacy…depends not merely on the extent to which principles of admissibility and significance intelligibly tell you what to look for and how to evaluate it, but also on how much evidence is necessary to justify an answer. Rational debate on determinacy--like rational debate on any subject whatsoever--cannot take place without reference to standards of proof. The problem is fundamental, and it is inescapable." Lawson, *Proving The Law*, 876-877 (emphasis added). See also, "The standard of proof is analogous to the preponderance of the evidence, the standard used in civil trials, as opposed to 'beyond a reasonable doubt', the standard in criminal trials." George Klosko, *Political Obligations*, (New York, NY, Oxford University, 2005), 22.

[14] Ibid. at 859 (parenthesis and emphasis added).

[15] Ibid. at 879 (emphasis added). See also, "People will generally deem it rational to require more and better evidence before taking action that could, if things go badly, result in incarceration for life than for action that could, if things go badly, result in nothing worse than a few moments of aggravation and lost time." Ibid. at 880.

[16] "There is always in litigation a margin of error, representing error in fact-finding, which both parties must take into account. Where one party has at stake an interest of transcending value--as a criminal defendant his liberty-- this margin of error is reduced as to him by the process of placing on the other party the burden . . . of persuading the fact finder at the conclusion of the trial of his guilt beyond a reasonable

doubt." *In re Winship*, 397 U.S. 358, 371-372 (U.S.N.Y. 1970) (Harlan, J., concurring).

[17] "Whoso killeth any person, the murderer shall be put to death by the mouth of witnesses: but one witness shall not testify against any person to cause him to die." Numbers 35:30 (kjv). See also, "Then shalt thou bring forth that man or that woman, which have committed that wicked thing, unto thy gates, even that man or that woman, and shalt stone them with stones, till they die. At the mouth of two witnesses, or three witnesses, shall he that is worthy of death be put to death; but at the mouth of one witness he shall not be put to death." Deuteronomy 17:5-6 (kjv). "One witness shall not rise up against a man for any iniquity, or for any sin, in any sin that he sinneth: at the mouth of two witnesses, or at the mouth of three witnesses, shall the matter be established." Deuteronomy 19:15 (kjv); "she wrote in the letters, saying, Proclaim a fast, and set Naboth on high among the people: And set two men, sons of Belial, before him, to bear witness against him, saying, Thou didst blaspheme God and the king. And then carry him out, and stone him, that he may die." 1Kings 21:9-10 (kjv).

[18] Matthew 18:16 (kjv) (emphasis added).

[19] "Whenever the fact finder is not satisfied that the available evidence meets the threshold for either truth or falsity with respect to a relevant proposition, leaving "I don't know" as the epistemologically appropriate answer, the law imposes the burden of that uncertainty upon someone, enabling the fact finder to render a decision in the case without necessarily fixing the legal truth value of the claim. Thus, when facts are at issue, the law specifies the requisite standards of proof and also prescribes a rule of decision for the zone of uncertainty in which those standards preclude a definitive true-or-false answer." Lawson, *Proving The Law*, 871.

[20] "So they read in the book in the law of God distinctly, and gave the sense, and caused them to understand the reading." Nehemiah 8:8 (kjv).

137

[21] Augustus Hopkins Strong, *Systematic Theology,* (Old Tappan, NJ, Fleming H. Revell Company, 1907), 4. "Theology has to do with subjective feelings only as they can be defined, and shown to be effective of objective truth upon the mind." Ibid., 14.

[22] Ibid. at 20.

[23] "My people are destroyed for lack of knowledge: because thou hast rejected knowledge, I will also reject thee, that thou shalt be no priest to me: seeing thou hast forgotten the law of thy God, I will also forget thy children." Hosea 4:6 (kjv).

[24] Matthew Henry, commenting on Matthew 6:19-24.

[25] "Let every man be fully persuaded in his own mind." Romans 14:5 (kjv).

[26] 2 Peter 1:20 (kjv).

[27] "Jesus said unto him, Thou shalt love the Lord thy God with all thy heart, and with all thy soul, and with all thy mind. This is the first and great commandment. And the second is like unto it, Thou shalt love thy neighbour as thyself. On these two commandments hang all the law and the prophets." Matthew 22:37-40 (kjv).

[28] "Doth not even nature itself teach you, that, if a man have long hair, it is a shame unto him?" How much more does nature teach us that self-defense is a right from God because life itself is the gift of God imparted to each and all, and no person has a right to take another person's life without just cause. The law itself was added/given to Israel because of man's violence towards other men. See, Galatians 3:19 (kjv); "The earth also was corrupt before God, and the earth was filled with violence." Genesis 6:11 (kjv). After this observation, God set to establish the nation of Israel to give them the "oracles of God". Romans 3:1-2 (kjv). See also, Psalm 147:19-20 (kjv).

[29] "For it seemeth to me unreasonable to send a prisoner, and not withal to signify the crimes laid against him." Acts 25:27 (kjv).

[30] See, Hebrews 5:12, 6:1 (kjv).

[31] Psalm 119:105 (kjv).

[32] "[T]he dark places of the earth are full of the habitations of cruelty." Psalm 74:20 (kjv). "Let their way be dark and slippery: and let the angel of the LORD persecute them." Psalm 35:6 (kjv). See also, 2 Peter 1:19, Luke 11:35-36, Micah 3:6, Amos 5:20, Ezekiel 32:7-8, Lamentations 3:6, Isaiah 29:15, Job 12:25 (kjv).

[33] Strong, *Systematic Theology,* 545.

[34] "If then God so clothe the grass, which is to day in the field, and to morrow is cast into the oven; how much more will he clothe you, O ye of little faith?" Luke 12:28 (kjv); "Know ye not that we shall judge angels? how much more things that pertain to this life?" 1 Corinthians 6:3 (kjv).

[35] Strong, *Systematic Theology*, 546.

[36] "Learn to do well; seek judgment; relieve the oppressed, judge the fatherless, plead for the widow." Isaiah 1:17 (kjv). See also, pastors are worthy of "double honor" by virtue of their relationship to the Church. "Let the elders that rule well be counted worthy of double honour, especially they who labour in the word and doctrine." 1 Timothy 5:17 (kjv).

[37] I Corinthians 9:9 (kjv).

[38] Mark 2:24 (kjv).

[39] Mark 2:27 (kjv).

[40] Mark 2:25-26 (kjv).

[41] "And it shall come to pass, *if ye diligently hearken unto me*, saith the LORD, to *bring in no burden through the gates of this city on the sabbath day*, but *hallow the sabbath day, to do no work therein*; Then shall there enter into the gates of this city kings and princes sitting upon the throne of David, riding in chariots and on horses, they, and their princes, the men of Judah, and the inhabitants of Jerusalem: and this city shall remain for ever." Jeremiah 17:24-25 (kjv) (emphasis added).

[42] Thou camest down also upon mount Sinai, and spakest with them from heaven, and gavest *them right judgments, and true laws, good statutes and commandments*: And *madest known unto them thy holy sabbath*, and commandedst them precepts, statutes, and laws, by the hand of Moses thy servant:" Nehemiah 9:14 (kjv) (emphasis added). "If thou *turn away* thy foot from the sabbath, *from doing thy pleasure on my holy day*; and call *the sabbath a delight*, the holy of the LORD, honourable; and shalt honour him, not doing thine own ways, nor finding thine own pleasure, nor speaking thine own words: Then shalt thou delight thyself in the LORD; and I will cause thee to ride upon the high places of the earth, and feed thee with the heritage of Jacob thy father: *for the mouth of the LORD hath spoken it.*" Isaiah 58:13-14 (kjv) (emphasis added).

[43] "*Thus saith the LORD*, Keep ye judgment, and do justice: for my salvation is near to come, and my righteousness to be revealed. Blessed is the man that doeth this, and the son of man that layeth hold on it; that *keepeth the sabbath from polluting it*, and keepeth his hand from doing any evil." Isaiah 56:1-2 (kjv) (emphasis added).

[44] "Remember me, O my God, concerning this, and *wipe not out my good deeds that I have done for the house of my God*, and for the offices thereof. In those days saw I in Judah some *treading wine presses on the sabbath*, and *bringing in sheaves, and lading asses*; as also wine, grapes, and figs, and all manner of burdens, which they brought into Jerusalem on the sabbath day: and *I testified against them* in the day wherein they sold victuals. There dwelt men of Tyre also therein, which *brought fish, and all manner of ware, and sold on the sabbath* unto the children of Judah, and in Jerusalem. Then I contended with the nobles of Judah, and said unto them, *What evil thing is this that ye do, and profane the sabbath day?*" Nehemiah 13:14-17 (kjv) (emphasis added). "Thus saith the LORD; Take heed to yourselves, and bear no burden on the sabbath day, nor bring it in by the gates of Jerusalem; Neither carry forth a burden out of your houses on the sabbath day,

neither do ye any work, but hallow ye the sabbath day, as I commanded your fathers." Jeremiah 17:21-22 (kjv).

[45] "And while the children of Israel were in the wilderness, they found a man that *gathered sticks upon the sabbath* day. And they that found him gathering sticks brought him unto Moses and Aaron, and unto all the congregation. And they put him in ward, because it was not declared what should be done to him. *And the LORD said unto Moses, The man shall be surely put to death*: all the congregation shall stone him with stones without the camp. And all the congregation brought him without the camp, and stoned him with stones, and he died; as the LORD commanded Moses." Numbers 15:32-36 (kjv) (emphasis added). Note: there was no factual trial to determine why he was picking sticks (e.g. to help a neighbor, out of necessity to cook food for his family, to facilitate worship, etc.). His violation was technical and the punishment was mandatory.

[46] Matthew Henry, commenting on Matthew 2:13-15 (kjv).

[47] Scriptures reveal the principle of necessity; that is, the law or rule changes where the facts require. Examples: "For the priesthood being changed, there is made of necessity a change also of the law." Hebrews 7:12 (kjv). "Now concerning virgins I have no commandment of the Lord: yet I give my judgment, as one that hath obtained mercy of the Lord to be faithful. I suppose therefore that this is good for the present distress, I say, that it is good for a man so to be...Nevertheless he that standeth stedfast in his heart, having no necessity, but hath power over his own will, and hath so decreed in his heart that he will keep his virgin, doeth well." 1 Corinthians 7:25-26, 37 (kjv).

[48] "And, behold, there was a man which had his hand withered. And they asked him, saying, Is it lawful to heal on the sabbath days? that they might accuse him. And he said unto them, What man shall there be among you, that shall have one sheep, and if it fall into a pit on the sabbath day, will he not lay hold on it, and lift it out? How much then is a man

better than a sheep? Wherefore it is lawful to do well on the sabbath days." Matthew 12:10-12 (kjv).

[49] "Abstain from all appearance of evil." 1 Thessalonians 5:22 (kjv).

[50] "Prove all things; hold fast that which is good." 1 Thessalonians 5:21 (kjv).

[51] "For when for the time ye ought to be teachers, ye have need that one teach you again which be the first principles of the oracles of God; and are become such as have need of milk, and not of strong meat. For every one that useth milk is unskilful in the word of righteousness: for he is a babe. But strong meat belongeth to them that are of full age, even those who by reason of use have their senses exercised to discern both good and evil." Hebrews 5:12-14 (kjv).

[52] "And he said unto them, This is that which the LORD hath said, To morrow is the rest of the holy sabbath unto the LORD: bake that which ye will bake to day, and seethe that ye will seethe; and that which remaineth over lay up for you to be kept until the morning. And they laid it up till the morning, as Moses bade: and it did not stink, neither was there any worm therein. And Moses said, Eat that to day; for to day is a sabbath unto the LORD: to day ye shall not find it in the field. Six days ye shall gather it; but on the seventh day, which is the sabbath, in it there shall be none. And it came to pass, that there went out some of the people on the seventh day for to gather, and they found none."

[53] Matthew Henry, commenting on Mark 2:25-26 (kjv).

[54] Ecclesiastes 7:16 (kjv).

[55] Matthew Henry, commenting on Ecclesiastes 7:16.

[56] "Now therefore hearken, O Israel, unto the statutes and unto the judgments, which I teach you, for to do them, that ye may live, and go in and possess the land which the LORD God of your fathers giveth you." Deuteronomy 4:1 (kjv). "[Jesus] said unto [the lawyer], What is written in the law? how readest thou? And he answering said, Thou shalt love the Lord thy

God with all thy heart, and with all thy soul, and with all thy strength, and with all thy mind; and thy neighbour as thyself. And he said unto him, Thou hast answered right: this do, and thou shalt live?" Luke 10:27-29 (kjv); "For the Son of man is not come to destroy men's lives, but to save them." Luke 9:56 (kjv).

[57] "And he reasoned in the synagogue every sabbath, and persuaded the Jews and the Greeks." Acts 18:4 (kjv). "See then that ye walk circumspectly, not as fools, but as wise, Redeeming the time, because the days are evil." Ephesians 5:15-16 (kjv). "Walk in wisdom toward them that are without, redeeming the time." Colossians 4:5 (kjv).

[58] Matthew 23:24 (kjv).

[59] Matthew 23:23 (kjv).

[60] Luke 6:7-9 (kjv) (emphasis added).

[61] "And the scribes and Pharisees brought unto him a woman taken in adultery; and when they had set her in the midst, They say unto him, Master, this woman was taken in adultery, in the very act. Now Moses in the law commanded us, that such should be stoned: but what sayest thou? This they said, tempting him, that they might have to accuse him. But Jesus stooped down, and with his finger wrote on the ground, as though he heard them not. So when they continued asking him, he lifted up himself, and said unto them, He that is without sin among you, let him first cast a stone at her." John 8:3-7 (kjv). See also, "And he charged them, saying, Take heed, beware of the leaven of the Pharisees, and of the leaven of Herod." Mark 8:15 (kjv).

[62] Kopel, *The Torah and Self-Defense*, 36.

[63] Matthew Henry, commenting on Luke 6:1-11.

[64] Randolph, *The Christian's Right to Bear Arms*, 37.

[65] "Behold my servant, whom I uphold; mine elect, in whom my soul delighteth; I have put my spirit upon him: he shall bring forth judgment to the Gentiles. He shall not cry, nor lift

up, nor cause his voice to be heard in the street. A bruised reed shall he not break, and the smoking flax shall he not quench: *he shall bring forth judgment unto truth.* He shall not fail nor be discouraged, till he have set judgment in the earth: and the isles shall wait for his law." Isaiah 42:1-4 (kjv) (emphasis added).

[66] Hebrews 2:14-15 (kjv).

[67] "Let the priests, the ministers of the LORD, weep between the porch and the altar, and let them say, *Spare thy people, O LORD, and give not thine heritage to reproach, that the heathen should rule over them:* wherefore should they say among the people, *Where is their God?*" Joel 2:17 (kjv) (emphasis added).

[68] Hebrews 7:1 (kjv).

[69] Kopel, *The Torah and Self-Defense*, 20.

[70] Ibid.

[71] Acts 3:25 (kjv). See also, Galatians 3:29 (kjv).

[72] "There was a little city, and few men within it; and there came a great king against it, and besieged it, and built great bulwarks against it". Ecclesiastes 9:14 (kjv). It is also a sign of a judged community. Matthew 24:49-51 (kjv).

[73] "Let the priests, the ministers of the LORD, weep between the porch and the altar, and let them say, *Spare thy people, O LORD, and give not thine heritage to reproach, that the heathen should rule over them:* wherefore should they say among the people, Where is their God?" Joel 2:17 (kjv) (emphasis added).

[74] "If my people, which are called by my name, shall humble themselves, and pray, and seek my face, and *turn from their wicked ways*; then will I hear from heaven, and will forgive their sin, and will heal their land." 2 Chronicles 7:14 (kjv) (emphasis added).

[75] Randolph, *The Christian's Right to Bear Arms*, 37.

[76] Matthew Henry, commenting on Hosea 7:8-16.

[77] "Bible passages are read through the lens of Jesus Christ's ministry that is thought...to focus on two key commandments that constitute what is known as the Summary of the Law: 'You shall love the Lord your God with all your heart, with all your soul, and with all your mind. This is the first and the great commandment. And the second is like it: You shall love your neighbor as yourself.'" Henry L. Chambers, *Biblical Interpretation, Constitutional Interpretation, and Ignoring Text*, Maryland Law Review, The Maryland Constitutional Law Schmooze (2009), 99. See also, all interpretations regarding the New Testament Church hold this same rule—meaning, if an action does not edify the Church, it cannot be claimed to come from God. 1 Corinthians chapter 14.

[78] Matthew 25:42-46 (kjv).

[79] Ibid. at verses 33-36, 40 (kjv).

[80] Matthew 22:36 (kjv).

[81] Ibid. at verse 38 (kjv).

[82] Ibid. at verse 39 (kjv).

[83] Mark 12:31 (kjv). In another passage Scripture records Jesus asking the lawyer how he interprets Scriptures. "[Jesus] said unto [a lawyer], What is written in the law? how readest thou? Thou shalt love the Lord thy God with all thy heart, and with all thy soul, and with all thy strength, and with all thy mind; and thy neighbour as thyself. And [Jesus] said unto [the lawyer], Thou hast answered right: this do, and thou shalt live." Luke 10:26-28 (kjv).

[84] "In the way of righteousness is life; and in the pathway thereof there is no death." Proverbs 12:28 (kjv).

[85] Ezekiel 18:11 (kjv) (emphasis added).

[86] Ibid. at 13 (kjv).

[87] See, Genesis 9:6 (kjv).

[88] "A man that doeth violence to the blood of any person shall flee to the pit; let no man stay him." Proverbs 28:17 (kjv).

[89] "Yea, a man may say, Thou hast faith, and I have works: shew me thy faith without thy works, and I will shew thee my faith by my works." James 2:18 (kjv). The works that show faith are those works Jesus demonstrates are done towards his neighbors. See, Matthew 25:33-36, 40 (kjv). See also, "But whoso hath this world's good, and seeth his brother have need, and shutteth up his bowels of compassion from him, how dwelleth the love of God in him?" 1 John 3:17 (kjv); "But when ye sin so against the brethren, and wound their weak conscience, ye sin against Christ." 1 Corinthians 8:12 (kjv).

[90] Strong, *Systematic Theology*, 35.

[91] "As also in all his epistles, speaking in them of these things; in which are some things hard to be understood, which they that are unlearned and unstable wrest, as they do also the other scriptures, unto their own destruction." 2 Peter 3:16 (kjv).

[92] See, Matthew Henry, commenting on 1 Samuel 24:1-8 (kjv), choosing to adopt an "interpretation [that] is more probable."

[93] Genesis 1:28 (kjv).

[94] Genesis 9:6 (kjv).

[95] Nehemiah 9:6; Job 7:20; Psalm 36:6, 104:29-30; Acts 17:28; Colossians 1:17; Hebrews 1:2-3; John 5:17; Genesis 2:2; Psalm 66:8-9; and 1 Timothy 6:13.

[96] "I know that, whatsoever God doeth, it shall be for ever: nothing can be put to it, nor any thing taken from it: and God doeth it, that men should fear before him." Ecclesiastes 3:14 (kjv). "Rejoicing in the habitable part of his earth; and my delights were with the sons of men." Proverbs 8:31 (kjv).

[97] Ephesians 5:29 (kjv) (emphasis added).

[98] Romans 13:9 (kjv) (emphasis added).

[99] Genesis 18:25 (kjv).

[100] The English word, "right", is the Hebrew word, mishpât (H4941), meaning "particular right".

[101] "As for God, his way is perfect". Psalm 18:30 (kjv).

[102] "[T]he Strength of Israel will not lie nor repent: for he is not a man, that he should repent." 1 Samuel 15:29 (kjv).

[103] Strong, *Systematic Theology*, 299 (emphasis added).

[104] Psalm 104:5 (kjv).

[105] Matthew Henry, commenting on Genesis 1:26-28.

[106] Ecclesiastes 7:7 (kjv)

[107] Romans 13:7 (kjv).

[108] 1Thessalonians 4:6 (kjv).

[109] Matthew Henry, commenting on Genesis 1:28 (kjv).

[110] Leviticus 25:18 (kjv). See also, "Save us, O God of our salvation, and *gather us together*, and *deliver us*". 1 Chronicles 16:35 (kjv) (emphasis added).

[111] Matthew Henry, commenting on Genesis 1:28 (kjv).

[112] See, Genesis 10:8-9 (kjv). "*He began to be a mighty one in the earth*, that is, whereas those that went before him were content to stand upon the same level with their neighbours, and though every man bore rule in his own house yet no man pretended any further, Nimrod's aspiring mind could not rest here; he was resolved to tower above his neighbours, not only to be eminent among them, but to lord it over them." Matthew Henry, commenting on Genesis 10:6-14.

[113] Lamentations 3:35, 36 (kjv).

[114] Psalm 9:4 (kjv).

[115] "And God said, Behold, I have given you every herb bearing seed, which is upon the face of all the earth, and every tree, in the which is the fruit of a tree yielding seed; to you it shall be for meat." Genesis 1:29 (kjv).

[116] "For there shall arise false Christs, and false prophets, and shall shew great signs and wonders; insomuch that, if it were possible, they shall deceive the very elect." Matthew 24:24 (kjv).

[117] Matthew Henry, commenting on Revelation 13:16-17 (emphasis added).

[118] 1 Corinthians 7:23 (kjv).

[119] Exodus 13:18 (asv). "[T]he text [of Exodus 13:18] shows that the Hebrews were marching out triumphantly as a free people, not running away like slaves." Kopel, *The Torah and Self-Defense*, 24.

[120] Kopel, *The Torah and Self-Defense*, 24.

[121] Ibid. at 25.

[122] 1 John 2:18 (kjv).

[123] 1 Peter 5:8-9 (kjv).

[124] 1 John 3:12 (kjv). See, "Ye are of your father the devil, and the lusts of your father ye will do. *He was a murderer from the beginning*". John 8:44 (kjv) (emphasis added).

[125] "Thou shalt have no other gods before me." Exodus 20:3 (kjv).

[126] "But strong meat belongeth to them that are of full age, even those who by reason of use have their senses exercised to discern both good and evil." Hebrews 5:14 (kjv).

[127] "Man that is in honour, and understandeth not, is like the beasts that perish." Psalm 49:20. See also, Psalm 73:22, 92:6 (kjv) and Ezekiel 45:9 (kjv).

[128] "For thou hast made him a little lower than the angels, and hast crowned him with glory and honour. Thou madest him to have dominion over the works of thy hands; thou hast put all things under his feet". Psalm 8:5-6 (kjv).

[129] Matthew Henry, commenting on Proverbs 1:1-6 (emphasis added).

[130] "And that we may be delivered from unreasonable and wicked men: for all men have not faith." 2 Thessalonians 3:2 (kjv).

[131] "Shall mortal man be more just than God? shall a man be more pure than his maker?" Job 4:17 (kjv).

[132] Proverbs 1:6 (kjv).

[133] Matthew 24:15 (kjv).

[134] "Therefore shall they eat of the fruit of their own way, and be filled with their own devices. For the turning away of the simple shall slay them, and the prosperity of fools shall destroy them." Proverbs 1:31-32 (kjv).

[135] See, Proverbs chapter 6.

[136] Lamentations 4:3 (kjv).

[137] Ibid.

[138] The New Testament cites the Old Testament throughout, including proverbs found in the books of Psalm and Proverbs. See, John 10:35 and James 4:6.

[139] "God set the members [of the body] every one of them...as it hath pleased him." 1 Corinthians 12:18 (kjv). "What *advantage* then hath the Jew? or what *profit* is there of circumcision? Much every way: chiefly, because that unto them were committed the oracles of God." Romans 3:1-2 (kjv) (emphasis added); "And at what instant I shall speak concerning a nation, and concerning a kingdom, *to build and to plant it*; If it do evil in my sight, that it obey not my voice, then I will *repent of the good*, wherewith I said I would *benefit them*." Jeremiah 18:9-10 (kjv) (emphasis added). See also, Hebrews chapter 6 (kjv). See also, "The God of heaven, he will prosper us; therefore we his servants will *arise and build*: but ye have no portion, nor right, nor memorial, in Jerusalem." Nehemiah 2:20 (kjv). God's general will for man is for them to "arise and build"; thus, they must enforce their "portion" and "right".

[140] "Meats for the belly, and the belly for meats: but God shall destroy both it and them. Now the body is not for fornication, but for the Lord; and the Lord for the body." 1 Corinthians 6:13 (kjv).

[141] Ibid.

[142] Christ hath *redeemed* us from the curse of the law, being made a curse for us: for it is written, Cursed is every one that hangeth on a tree." Galatians 3:13 (kjv). "Redeemed" (exagorazō, G1805) means, "improve opportunity". The same word is used in Ephesians 5:16, Colossians 4:5, and Galatians 4:5.

[143] "But when the fulness of the time was come, God sent forth his Son, made of a woman, made under the law, To redeem [improve, exagorazō, G1805] them that were under the law, that we might receive the adoption of sons...Wherefore thou art no more a servant, but a son; and if a son, then an heir of God through Christ." Galatians 4:4-5, 7 (kjv).

[144] "[I]n the image of God made he man". Genesis 1:27 (kjv).

[145] Galatians 3:13 (kjv).

[146] From the beginning of Creation, God's standard for man was goodness, not destruction. "And God saw every thing that he had made, and, behold, it was very good." Genesis 1:31 (kjv); "And the LORD God said, It is not good that the man should be alone; I will make him an help meet for him." Genesis 2:18 (kjv); "But as for you, ye thought evil against me; but God meant it unto good, to bring to pass, as it is this day, to save much people alive." Genesis 50:20 (kjv); "It is a good land which the LORD our God doth give us." Deuteronomy 1:25 (kjv).

[147] "Ye shall therefore keep all my statutes, and all my judgments, and do them: that the land, whither I bring you to dwell therein, spue you not out." Leviticus 20:22 (kjv).

[148] "The earth also was corrupt before God, and the earth was filled with violence. And God looked upon the earth, and, behold, it was corrupt; for all flesh had corrupted his way

upon the earth." Genesis 6:11-12 (kjv). "If a soul sin, and commit a trespass against the LORD...in a thing taken away by violence...[t]hen it shall be, because he hath sinned, and is guilty, that he shall restore that which he took violently away". Leviticus 6:2,4 (kjv). "He shall spare the poor and needy, and shall save the souls of the needy. He shall redeem their soul from deceit and violence: and precious shall their blood be in his sight." Psalm 72:13-14 (kjv). "So ye shall not pollute the land wherein ye are: for blood it defileth the land: and the land cannot be cleansed of the blood that is shed therein, but by the blood of him that shed it." Numbers 35:33 (kjv).

[149] See, Romans 13:1-4 (kjv).

[150] "Wherein the king granted the Jews which were in every city to gather themselves together, and to stand for their life, to destroy, to slay, and to cause to perish, all the power of the people and province that would assault them, both little ones and women, and to take the spoil of them for a prey". Esther 8:11 (kjv).

[151] "All scripture is given by inspiration of God, and is profitable for doctrine, for reproof, for correction, for instruction in righteousness". 2 Timothy 3:16 (kjv).

[152] Matthew 5:12 (kjv) (emphasis added).

[153] Matthew 5:13 (kjv).

[154] See also, Hebrews chapter 11.

[155] "And the Sabeans fell upon them, and took them away; yea, they have slain the servants with the edge of the sword; and I only am escaped alone to tell thee." Job 1:15 (kjv).

[156] Job 19:29 (kjv).

[157] See, 1 Timothy 2:1-2 (kjv).

[158] Lamentations 3:31-36 (kjv) (emphasis added).

[159] Matthew 5:17 (kjv).

[160] Matthew 5:19 (kjv).

[161] "Verily I say unto you, Inasmuch as ye have done it unto one of the least of these my brethren, ye have done it unto me." Matthew 25:40 (kjv).

[162] "And now abideth faith, hope, charity, these three; but the greatest of these is charity." 1 Corinthians 13:13 (kjv). "Thou shalt love thy neighbour as thyself. There is none other commandment greater than these." Mark 12:31 (kjv).

[163] "Greater love hath no man than this, that a man lay down his life for his friends." John 15:13 (kjv).

[164] Romans 13:10 (kjv).

[165] Hebrews 11:25 (kjv). See also, "It seemed good unto us, being assembled with one accord, to send chosen men unto you with our beloved Barnabas and Paul, Men that have hazarded their lives for the name of our Lord Jesus Christ." Acts 15:25-26 (kjv).

[166] See, James 5:6 (kjv).

[167] Hebrews 11:32-34 (kjv).

[168] Matthew 18:7 (kjv).

[169] Ibid.

[170] The mark of a cursed person is this: "thy life shall hang in doubt before thee; and thou shalt fear day and night, and shalt have none assurance of thy life." Deuteronomy 28:66 (kjv). See also, King David notes that those who kill innocent people in their own home are much more worthy of retribution. "How much more, when wicked men have slain a righteous person in his own house upon his bed? shall I not therefore now require his blood of your hand, and take you away from the earth?" 2 Samuel 4:11 (kjv).

[171] Ephesians 5:16 (kjv).

[172] "But if any provide not for his own, and specially for those of his own house, he hath denied the faith, and is worse than an infidel." 1 Timothy 5:8 (kjv). The duty of protecting "his own" and "his own house" imply that the duty extends to

family and those one has a social relationship with, such as neighbors, community, and State.

[173] "Whether Paul, or Apollos, or Cephas, or the world, or life, or death, or things present, or things to come; all are yours; And ye are Christ's; and Christ is God's." I Corinthians 3:22-23 (kjv).

[174] "They say unto him, Caesar's. Then saith he unto them, Render therefore unto Caesar the things which are Caesar's; and unto God the things that are God's." Matthew 22:21 (kjv).

[175] "Ye are bought with a price; be not ye the servants of men." 1 Corinthians 7:23 (kjv).

[176] The word "speak" in the English comes from the Hebrew word, "dâbar" (H1696). The same word is used in Psalm 47:3 ("He shall subdue the people under us, and the nations under our feet) and Psalm 18:47 ("It is God that avengeth me, and subdueth the people under me").

[177] Matthew Henry, commenting on Psalm 127:1-5.

[178] Kopel, *The Torah and Self-Defense*, 25, quoting Eric Voegelin, a historian of philosophy.

[179] "I have seen the foolish taking root: but suddenly I cursed his habitation. His children are far from safety, and they are crushed in the gate, neither is there any to deliver them." Job 5:3-4 (kjv). "Like as a father pitieth his children, so the LORD pitieth them that fear him. Psalm 103:13 (kjv). "[God] hath strengthened the bars of thy gates; he hath blessed thy children within thee. He maketh peace in thy borders". Psalm 147:13-14 (kjv). "A good man leaveth an inheritance to his children's children: and the wealth of the sinner is laid up for the just." Proverbs 13:22 (kjv). "In the fear of the LORD is strong confidence: and his children shall have a place of refuge." Proverbs 14:26 (kjv). See also, Lamentation chapter 4. "And he shall turn the heart of the fathers to the children, and the heart of the children to their fathers, lest I come and smite the earth with a curse." Malachi 4:6 (kjv).

[180] Strong, *Systematic Theology*, 27,

[181] Ibid. at 33.

[182] Mark 7:13 (kjv).

[183] Acts 7:25 (kjv).

[184] See, Exodus chapter 1.

[185] Matthew 18:6-7 (kjv).

[186] Matthew Henry, commenting on Psalm 12:1-8.

[187] "The LORD executeth righteousness and judgment for all that are oppressed." Psalm 103:6 (kjv).

[188] Exodus 2:14 (kjv).

[189] Proverbs 3:30 (kjv).

[190] Proverbs 12:24 (kjv).

[191] Strong, *Systematic Theology*, 15.

[192] Ibid., citing Origen.

[193] Ibid.

[194] "But thou, O Daniel, shut up the words, and seal the book, even to the time of the end: many shall run to and fro, and *knowledge shall be increased*." Daniel 12:4 (kjv) (emphasis added).

[195] "And the times of this ignorance God winked at; but now commandeth all men every where to repent". Acts 17:30 (kjv).

[196] Ibid., citing Martineau, Essays, 1 : 29, 40; Am. Theol. Rev., 1859: 101-126—art. On the Idea, Sources and Uses of Christian Theology.

[197] George Hegel, *Philosophy of Right*, Trnsl. T.M. Knox, Compiled in *Great Books of the Western* World, (reprinted by Oxford University Press, William Benton, 1952), 28 (emphasis added).

[198] Ibid. at 107.

[199] Ibid.

[200] Ibid. at 80.

[201] Ibid. at 86.

[202] "When individuals, holding religious views in common, form themselves into a church, a Corporation, they fall under the general control and oversight of the higher state officials." Ibid. at 87.

[203] "But now hath he obtained a more excellent ministry, by how much also he is the mediator of a better covenant, which was established upon better promises." Hebrews 8:6 (kjv).

[204] Matthew 22:21, Mark 12:17 and Luke 20:25.

[205] John 11:47 (kjv).

[206] "And Samson took hold of the two middle pillars upon which the house stood, and on which it was borne up, of the one with his right hand, and of the other with his left. And Samson said, Let me die with the Philistines. And he bowed himself with all his might; and the house fell upon the lords, and upon all the people that were therein. So the dead which he slew at his death were more than they which he slew in his life." Judges 16:29-30 (kjv).

[207] 2 Peter 1:18-20 (kjv).

[208] Luke 22:49 (kjv).

[209] John 18:10-11 (kjv).

[210] Matthew 26:52 (kjv).

[211] Matthew 26:54 (kjv).

[212] John 18:11 (kjv).

[213] Matthew 26:53 (kjv).

[214] John 10:10 (kjv).

[215] See, Romans 6:10 (kjv).

[216] Luke 22:37-38 (kjv) (emphasis added).

[217] Jesus confirms that those who teach people to break the law are least in the kingdom. "Whoever therefore breaks one of the commandments, and teaches men so, shall be called least in the kingdom of heaven." (Matthew 5:19). The Old Testament confirms the right of self-defense. Therefore, an interpretation taught contrary to self-defense is error.

[218] Kopel, *The Human Right Of Self-Defense*, 107.

[218] Ibid. at 45.

[219] Ibid. at 107-108.

[220] Randolph, *The Christians' Right to Bear Arms*, 39.

[221] Genesis 27:40 (kjv).

[222] Matthew Henry, commenting on Genesis 27:30-40.

[223] "In his days Edom revolted from under the hand of Judah, and made a king over themselves." 2 Kings 8:20 (kjv).

[224] Habakkuk 2:7-8 (kjv). See also, "Violence is risen up into a rod of wickedness: none of them shall remain, nor of their multitude, nor of any of theirs: neither shall there be wailing for them." Ezekiel 7:11 (kjv).

[225] Isaiah 14:12-20 (kjv).

[226] 1 Peter 5:8-9 (kjv).

[227] "If I have rewarded evil unto him that was at peace with me; (yea, I have delivered him that without cause is mine enemy:) Let the enemy persecute my soul, and take it; yea, let him tread down my life upon the earth, and lay mine honour in the dust. Selah." Psalm 7:4-5 (kjv).

[228] Kopel, *The Human Right Of Self-Defense*, 111.

[229] Luke 22:35-36 (kjv).

[230] "Behold, I send you forth as sheep in the midst of wolves: be ye therefore wise as serpents, and harmless as doves." Matthew 10:16 (kjv).

[231] "For ye have the poor always with you; but me ye have not always." Matthew 26:11 (kjv).

[232] John 18:3-6 (kjv) (emphasis added).

[233] Revelation 2:16 (kjv).

[234] Matthew 8:5-13 (kjv).

[235] Randolph, *Christian's Right to Bear Arms*, 36.

[236] Ibid. at 31.

[237] Matthew 11:11 (kjv); Mark 1:3 (kjv).

[238] Luke 3:13 (kjv).

[239] Luke 3:12-14 (kjv).

[240] "Giovanni...point[s] out that [the theory of just war] permit[s] the defense of one's own body and further, that not only]one's individual and private body' may be defended with arms, but also the mystical body of which one is a part [i.e. the State]." Jasonne Grabher O'Brien, *In Defense of the Mystical Body: Giovanni da Legnano's Theory of Reprisals*, (2002), 31 (found at http://romanlegaltradition.org/contents/2002/RLT-OBRIEN1.PDF).

[241] "For a thousand years, the Twelve Tables were venerated as the embodiment of Roman law. For example, they were held in the highest esteem by the great Roman lawyer and orator of the first century BC, Cicero." Kopel, *The Human Right Of Self-Defense*, 110. "The self-defense rules are in Table VIII: 12. If a theft be committed at night, and the thief be killed, let his death be deemed lawful. 13. If in the daytime (only if he defend himself with weapons). The Twelve Tables thus contained a counterpart of the Hebrew law from Exodus, based on the principle that the slaying of a night-time burglar was lawful, because the burglar was presumed to be a deadly threat. A daytime burglar could also be slain, if the facts indicated that he were a deadly threat." Ibid. at 109.

[242] Kopel, *The Torah and Self-Defense*, 27, citing scholar Philo of Alexandria who wrote between approximately 20 B.C. to 50 A.D.

[243] Marcus Tullius Cicero, *Orations of Marcus Tullius Cicero*, Trnsl. Charles Duke Yonge, Revised Ed. (Colonial Press, 1900), 204

[244] Marcus Tullius Cicero, *The Orations of Marcus Tullius Cicero*, Vol. 1, Compiler unknown, Translated into English (London, 1741), 278. See also, "There is one rule which endures forever, to maintain one's safety by any and every means." Marcus Tullius Cicero, *On Invention* (De inventione) (84 BC) (bk. 2, ch. 22) ("invention" means "the construction of arguments")

[245] Ibid.

[246] Ibid. at 112.

[247] God instructs Israel to be ready for war but does not instruct them on the details of when war is required: that is determined on a circumstantial basis. "Under Moses and Joshua the Jews repelled the assaults of the Amalekites, Ex. XVII:8 acts which God had not before commanded but afterward approved." Randolph, *Christian's Right to Bear Arms*, 6. "Then came Amalek, and fought with Israel in Rephidim. And Moses said unto Joshua, Choose us out men, and go out, fight with Amalek: to morrow I will stand on the top of the hill with the rod of God in mine hand. So Joshua did as Moses had said to him, and fought with Amalek: and Moses, Aaron, and Hur went up to the top of the hill." Exodus 17:8-10 (kjv).

[248] "The right of the people to keep and bear arms, shall not be infringed". U.S., Amend., II. "That every citizen has a right to bear arms in defense of himself and the State". Alabama, I, 28; Conn., I, 17; ["every person has", etc.] Michigan, XVIII, 7. "The citizens of this State shall have the right to keep and bear arms for their common defense" Arkansas, I, 5. "The people shall the right to bear arms in defense of themselves and of the lawful authority of the State". Florida, Declaration of Rights,

22. "The people shall have the right to bear arms for the defense of themselves and the State". Indiana, I, 82; Oregon, I, 28; Vermont, Part I, 16. "That the rights of the citizens to bear arms in defense of themselves and the State shall not be questioned; but the General Assembly may pass laws to prevent persons from carrying concealed arms". Kentucky, XIII, 25. "The people have the right to bear arms for their defense and security". Kansas, Bill of Rights, 4. "Every citizen has a right to keep and bear arms for the common defense; and this right shall never be questioned". Maine, I, 16. "The people have a right to keep and bear arms for the common defense". Massachusetts, Part 1, 17; South Carolina, I, 28. "And that their right to bear arms in defense of themselves, and of the lawful authority of the State, cannot be questioned". Missouri, I, 8. "All persons shall have a right to keep and bear arms fur their defense". Mpi., I, 15. "The right of the people to keep and bear arms shall not be infringed". North Carolina, I, 24; Rhode Island, I, 22; [but the General Assembly shall have power to prescribe by law the manner in which arms may be borne,] (Georgia, 1, 14). "That the right of the citizens to bear arms in defense of themselves and the State shall not be questioned". Pennsylvania, IX, 21. "That the citizens of this State have a right to keep and to bear arms for their common defense. But the Legislature shall have power, by law, to regulate the wearing of arms with a view to prevent crime". Term., I, 20. "Every person shall have the right to keep and bear arms, in the lawful defense of himself or the State, under such regulations as the Legislature may prescribe". Texas, I, 13. Franklin Hough, *American Constitutions*, Vol. 2, (Albany, NY, Weed, Parsons & Co., 1972), 598-599.

[249] The Jews spread throughout Europe because of persecution, which began as follows: "at that time there was a great persecution against the church which was at Jerusalem; and they were all scattered abroad throughout the regions of Judaea and Samaria, except the apostles." Acts 8:1 (kjv).

[250] "The great British historian Lord Acton wrote that 'the greater part of the political ideas' of John Milton and John Locke 'may be found in the ponderous Latin of Jesuits who

were subjects of the Spanish Crown . . . .' such as Suárez. Suárez was also a major influence on [Hugo] Grotius." Ibid., 72, discussing how Jewish philosophers influenced the philosophy of Western Civilization.

[251] Kopel, *The Torah and Self-Defense*, 28.

[252] Ibid. at 70, discussing Roman philosopher Pierino Belli.

[253] Ibid.

[254] Ibid. (emphasis added).

[255] Kopel, *The Torah And Self-Defense*, 40-41.

[256] Matthew 15:3-6 (kjv).

[257] Matthew 5:21-22 (kjv) (emphasis added).

[258] "Strive not with a man without cause, if he have done thee no harm." Proverbs 3:30 (kjv). See also, Psalm 35:19 (kjv); Proverbs 1:11, 24:8 (kjv).

[259] Kopel, *The Torah and Self-Defense*, 42.

[260] Addressing the more technical matter of interpreting what Jesus was teaching, notice the kind of slap Jesus describes: "whosoever shall smite thee on thy right cheek". Jesus' use of "right cheek" is significant to the interpretation. Most people were and are right handed either naturally or through training—especially in biblical days and even today in the Middle East (of the many thousands of people in Israel, only 700 hundred were left handed. See, Judges 20:15-16). If someone were to use his right hand to "smite" a person in the face, he would slap that person on the left side of his face. This is significant to understanding Jesus' instructions of "turning the cheek". The normal way a person is struck on the right side of the cheek is for the offender to use a backhand approach. This approach is akin to a spit in the face—an insult, but not a formidable attack upon a person's life or limb. By specific description of Jesus' statement, turning the other cheek necessarily does not include an attack on one's life.

[261] Matthew 5:5 (kjv).

[262] Psalm 115:16 (kjv).

[263] Matthew Henry, commenting on Matthew 5:5 (emphasis added).

[264] "When God arose to judgment, to save all the meek of the earth. Selah." Psalm 76:9 (kjv). "But let him that glorieth glory in this, that he understandeth and knoweth me, that I am the LORD which exercise lovingkindness, judgment, and righteousness, in the earth: for in these things I delight, saith the LORD." Jeremiah 9:24 (kjv). "Then will I also confess unto thee that thine own right hand can save thee." Job 40:14 (kjv).

[265] Psalm 37:32 (kjv).

[266] Psalm 37:33 (kjv).

[267] Matthew Henry, commenting on Matthew 5:3.

[268] Job 27:13-15 (kjv).

[269] Job 27:23 (kjv).

[270] Psalm 109:7 (kjv).

[271] "And it came to pass in those days, when Moses was grown, that he went out unto his brethren, and looked on their burdens: and he spied an Egyptian smiting an Hebrew, one of his brethren. And he looked this way and that way, and when he saw that there was no man, he slew the Egyptian, and hid him in the sand." Exodus 2:11-12 (kjv).

[272] "Now the priest of Midian had seven daughters: and they came and drew water, and filled the troughs to water their father's flock. And the shepherds came and drove them away: but Moses stood up and helped them, and watered their flock." Exodus 2:16-17 (kjv).

[273] "Moses' confrontation with the evil shepherds has been universally praised by commentators." Kopel, *The Torah and Self-Defense*, 23.

[274] "Surely oppression maketh a wise man mad". Ecclesiastes 7:7 (kjv).

[275] "Because to every purpose there is time and judgment, therefore the misery of man is great upon him." Ecclesiastes 8:6 (kjv).

[276] "He delivered me from my strong enemy, and from them that hated me: for they were too strong for me." 2 Samuel 22:18 (kjv). James 5:6 (kjv). See also, "But ye have despised the poor. Do not rich men oppress you, and draw you before the judgment seats?" James 2:6 (kjv).

[277] "Where the word of a king is, there is power: and who may say unto him, What doest thou?" Ecclesiastes 8:4 (kjv).

[278] See, Genesis chapter 14. See also, "Wherefore I have not sinned against thee, but thou doest me wrong to war against me: the LORD the Judge be judge this day between the children of Israel and the children of Ammon." Judges 11:27 (kjv).

[279] "For how can I endure to see the evil that shall come unto my people? or how can I endure to see the destruction of my kindred?" Esther 8:6 (kjv). See also, "They that forsake the law praise the wicked: but such as keep the law contend with them." Proverbs 28:4 (kjv).

[280] "He striketh them as wicked men in the open sight of others; Because they turned back from him, and would not consider any of his ways: So that they cause the cry of the poor to come unto him, and he heareth the cry of the afflicted. When he giveth quietness, who then can make trouble? and when he hideth his face, who then can behold him? whether it be done against a nation, or against a man only: That the hypocrite reign not, lest the people be ensnared." Job 34:26-30 (kjv).

[281] "The wicked have drawn out the sword, and have bent their bow, to cast down the poor and needy, and to slay such as be of upright conversation. Their sword shall enter into their own heart, and their bows shall be broken."

[282] Exodus 2:11 (kjv).

[283] "God led the people about, by the way of the wilderness by the Red Sea: and the children of Israel went up armed out of the land of Egypt." Exodus 13:18 (asv).

[284] Kopel, *The Torah and Self-Defense*, 23

[285] "And, behold, there appeared unto them Moses and Elias talking with him." Matthew 17:3 (kjv).

[286] Strong, *Systematic Theology*, 546.

[287] Lamentations 3:33-36 (kjv) (emphasis added).

[288] mishpât, H4941.

[289] Genesis 18:25 (kjv).

[290] Matthew Henry, commenting on Matthew 5:39 (kjv).

[291] Exodus 21:22 (kjv).

[292] Exodus 21:26 (kjv); Leviticus 24:20 (kjv); and Deuteronomy 19:21 (kjv).

[293] Genesis 9:6 (kjv). See also, Leviticus 24:17 (kjv).

[294] Matthew Henry, commenting of Matthew 5:38.

[295] Matthew 4:43-44 (kjv).

[296] "Thou shalt not hate thy brother in thine heart: thou shalt in any wise rebuke thy neighbour, and not suffer sin upon him. Thou shalt not avenge, nor bear any grudge against the children of thy people, but thou shalt love thy neighbour as thyself: I am the LORD." Leviticus 19:17-18 (kjv). "If thou meet thine enemy's ox or his ass going astray, thou shalt surely bring it back to him again." Exodus 23:4 (kjv). "Rejoice not when thine enemy falleth, and let not thine heart be glad when he stumbleth: Lest the LORD see it, and it displease him, and he turn away his wrath from him." Proverbs 24:17-18 (kjv). See also, Leviticus 19:10, 33-34; 24:22; 25:35 (kjv); Numbers 15:16 (kjv); Deuteronomy 10:19 (kjv).

[297] "Say not thou, I will recompense evil; but wait on the LORD, and he shall save thee". Proverbs 20:22 (kjv); "Say not, I will do so to him as he hath done to me: I will render to

the man according to his work." Proverbs 24:29 (kjv); "If thine enemy be hungry, give him bread to eat; and if he be thirsty, give him water to drink: For thou shalt heap coals of fire upon his head, and the LORD shall reward thee." Proverbs 25:21-22 (kjv).

[298] Matthew 5:13 (kjv).

[299] See, Matthew 19:19 (kjv), Matthew 22:39 (kjv), Mark 12:31 (kjv), Luke 10:27 (kjv), Romans 13:9 (kjv), Galatians 5:14 (kjv) and James 2:8 (kjv).

[300] Matthew 5:45 (kjv).

[301] See, 1 Corinthians 15:55-57 (kjv).

[302] "For in that [Jesus] died, he died unto sin once: but in that he liveth, he liveth unto God." Romans 6:10 (kjv).

[303] "Hereby perceive we the love of God, because he laid down his life for us: and we ought to lay down our lives for the brethren." 1 John 3:16 (kjv).

[304] Compare, "Ye have heard that it was said by them *of old time*". Matthew 5:21 (kjv).

[305] Compare, Matthew 26:31 (kjv).

[306] See, John 8:1-7 (kjv).

[307] Jesus was not undermining the law itself but expected that judges would render righteous judgment. "There was in a city a judge, which feared not God, neither regarded man" Luke 18:2 (kjv).

[308] Matthew 23:23 (kjv).

[309] Mark 8:15 (kjv).

[310] Romans 13:14 (kjv).

[311] "Go not forth hastily to strive, lest thou know not what to do in the end thereof, when thy neighbour hath put thee to shame. Debate thy cause with thy neighbour himself; and discover not a secret to another: Lest he that heareth it put thee

to shame, and thine infamy turn not away." Proverbs 25:8-10 (kjv).

[312] "They rewarded me evil for good to the *spoiling of my soul*." Psalm 35:12 (kjv). See also, "In those days there was no king in Israel, but every man did that which was right in his own eyes." Judges 17:6 (kjv). "There was no magistrate in the land, that might put them to shame in any thing". Judges 18:7, 21:25 (kjv).

[313] (1) man towards his government (Romans chapter 13), (2) man towards his enemies (Romans chapter 12), and (3) man towards his friends (Romans chapter 15).

[314] Romans chapter 12: "Be not overcome of evil, but overcome evil with good" verse 21). Romans chapter 13: "For he is the minister of God to thee for good" (verse 4). Romans chapter 15: "Let every one of us please his neighbour for his good to edification" (verse 2). It is absurd to say that any action towards man, including government, is unlimited and ignores the fundamental right of man: preservation and protection.

[315] Cp. Romans 13:1 and Romans 15:2. If self-defense rejecters teach that Romans 13:1 teaches submission to government is unlimited, do they teach that Romans 15:2 teaches that one give all he owns to a neighbor who does not help himself? Scriptures expressly limit "pleasing neighbor" by these principles: "Withhold not good from them to whom it is due, *when it is in the power of thine hand to do it*." Proverbs 3:27 (kjv). "[I]f any would not work, neither should he eat." 2 Thessalonians 3:10 (kjv). Principles limiting "pleasing neighbor: (1) when it is in your power, and (2) when the neighbor is not slothful.

[316] "If there be a controversy between men, and they come unto judgment, that the judges may judge them; then they shall justify the righteous, and condemn the wicked" Deuteronomy 25:1 (kjv). The root of the need for society is that individuals will always judge their own cause in their favor; thus, there

must be a neutral authority to discern the matter of right. See, Proverbs 18:17 (kjv).

[317] American Declaration of Independence, July 4, 1776, found at *The Declaration of Independence, 1776* (Washington D.C., Department of State, 1911), 3-4.

[318] James Madison, "Federalist Paper 53," in *The Federalist Papers: A Collection of Essays in Favour of the Constitution,* Alexander Hamilton, John Jay, and James Madison (Birmingham, AL: Cliff Road Books, 2006), 411 (emphasis added). Hereinafter, all Federalist Papers are referenced from this source and will be cited using the author's name, federalist paper number and the book page number.

[319] James 4:17 (kjv).

[320] "He fashioneth their hearts alike; he considereth all their works." Psalm 33:15 (kjv). See also, Ch. 2., Maxim 3, Natural Rights Serves as Basis for Human Compassion.

[321] Commenting on Deuteronomy 10:12 (kjv), "And now, Israel, what doth the LORD thy God require of thee, but to fear the LORD thy God, to walk in all his ways, and to love him, and to serve the LORD thy God with all thy heart and with all thy soul".

[322] "I will praise thee; for I am fearfully and wonderfully made: marvellous are thy works; and that my soul knoweth right well." Psalm 139:14 (kjv).

[323] "Without understanding, covenantbreakers, *without natural affection*, implacable, unmerciful: Who knowing the judgment of God, that they which commit such things are *worthy of death*, not only do the same, but have pleasure in them that do them." Romans 1:31-32 (kjv) (emphasis added).

[324] "Therefore leaving the principles of the doctrine of Christ, let us go on unto perfection; not laying again the foundation of repentance from dead works, and of faith toward God". Hebrews 6:1 (kjv).

[325] (Emphasis added). See also, "Did not he that made me in the womb make him? and did not one fashion us in the womb?" Job 31:15 (kjv).

[326] See, Romans chapter 13. See, *Romans 13: The True Meaning of Submission*, (Liberty Defense League, Kalispell, MT, 2011), www.romans13truth.com.

[327] Job 31:22 (kjv).

[328] "O LORD my God, if I have done this; if there be iniquity in my hands; If I have rewarded evil unto him that was at peace with me; (yea, I have delivered him that without cause is mine enemy:) Let the enemy persecute my soul, and take it; yea, *let him tread down my life upon the earth, and lay mine honour in the dust.* Selah." Psalm 7:2-5. (kjv) (emphasis added).

[329] See, Matthew 3:7, 12:34, 23:33 and Luke 3:7.

[330] Matthew 23:23 (kjv).

[331] John 2:15 (kjv).

[332] See also, "Depart from evil, and do good; seek peace, and pursue it." Psalm 34:14 (kjv).

[333] Ezekiel 18:11 (kjv); Psalm 37:37 (kjv).

[334] Jeremiah 8:11, 15 (kjv).

[335] Jeremiah 7:5-7 (kjv).

[336] Stanton, C.A., *The Friend*: A Religious and Literary Journal, "War is Unlawful Under the Gospel Dispensation", Volume 78, November 12, 1904, (Philadelphia, PA, WM. H. Pile's Sons, 1905), 141, 142.

[337] Ibid., 142.

[338] "He preserveth not the life of the wicked: but giveth right to the poor." Job 36:6 (kjv).

[339] "And the work of righteousness shall be peace; and the effect of righteousness quietness and assurance for ever." Isaiah 32:17 (kjv). See also, 1 Timothy 2:1-2 (kjv).

[340] See, Romans 11:24 (kjv) where things "contrary to nature" are used to illustrate spiritual truths.

[341] Romans 14:7 (kjv).

[342] John 2:15.

[343] See also, Proverbs 3:29 (kjv).

[344] "One law shall be to him that is homeborn, and unto the stranger that sojourneth among you." Exodus 12:49 (kjv). "Ye shall have one manner of law, as well for the stranger, as for one of your own country: for I am the LORD your God." Leviticus 24:22 (kjv).

[345] Judgment must be based upon true evidence: "Neither shalt thou bear false witness against thy neighbour." Deuteronomy 5:20 (kjv). Judges must seek the truth in trial: "And the judges shall make diligent inquisition: and, behold, if the witness be a false witness, and hath testified falsely against his brother". Deuteronomy 19:18 (kjv). Sentencing must be proportional to the crime: "And if any mischief follow, then thou shalt give life for life, Eye for eye, tooth for tooth, hand for hand, foot for foot". Exodus 21:23-24 (kjv). Criminal trials must be speedy: "Because sentence against an evil work is not executed speedily, therefore the heart of the sons of men is fully set in them to do evil." Ecclesiastes 8:11 (kjv). Evidence must be sufficient to overcome burden of proof (i.e. presumption of innocence): "At the mouth of two witnesses, or three witnesses, shall he that is worthy of death be put to death; but at the mouth of one witness he shall not be put to death." Deuteronomy 17:6 (kjv).

[346] Democracy is purely defined as a State where political power rests in the people. There is a difference between a democracy in nature and in administration. A democracy in administration means that the individuals in that State administer all of the laws, while a democracy in nature that is administered by representatives under constitutional constraints is known as a Republic.

[347] Matthew Henry, commenting on 2 Kings 24:20.

[348] Isaiah 3:5 (kjv). See also, "Take ye heed every one of his neighbour, and trust ye not in any brother: for every brother will utterly supplant, and every neighbour will walk with slanders. And they will deceive every one his neighbour, and will not speak the truth: they have taught their tongue to speak lies, and weary themselves to commit iniquity." Jeremiah 9:4-5 (kjv).

[349] "I exhort therefore, that, first of all, supplications, prayers, intercessions, and giving of thanks, be made for all men; For kings, and for all that are in authority; that we may lead a quiet and peaceable life in all godliness and honesty." 1 Timothy 2:1-3 (kjv). "They have set up kings, *but not by me*: they have made princes, and I knew it not: of their silver and their gold have they made them idols, that they may be cut off." Hosea 8:4 (kjv) (emphasis added).

[350] "For men verily swear by the greater: and an oath for confirmation is to them an end of all strife." Hebrews 6:16 (kjv). See also, "Though it be but a man's covenant, yet if it be confirmed, no man disannulleth, or added thereto." Galatians 3:15 (kjv). "My covenant will I not break". Psalm 89:34 (kjv).

[351] "And your covenant with death shall be disannulled, and your agreement with hell shall not stand." Isaiah 28:18 (kjv).

[352] Genesis 6:11 (kjv).

[353] See also, "An evil man seeketh only rebellion: therefore a cruel messenger shall be sent against him." A true rebel is someone who revolts against the peace of man.

[354] "Therefore my people are gone into captivity, because they *have no knowledge*". Isaiah 5:13 (kjv) (emphasis added).

[355] Judges 20:1, 11 (kjv).

[356] Deuteronomy 19:12 (kjv).

[357] See also, "Cursed be he that smiteth his neighbour secretly. And all the people shall say, Amen." Deuteronomy 27:24 (kjv).

[358] Kopel, *The Torah and Self-Defense*, 28.

[359] "Thus saith the Lord GOD; Let it suffice you, O princes of Israel: remove violence and spoil, and execute judgment and justice, take away your exactions from my people, saith the Lord GOD." Ezekiel 45:9 (kjv). "He that justifieth the wicked, and he that condemneth the just, even they both are abomination to the LORD." Proverbs 17:15 (kjv).

[360] "Egypt shall be a desolation, and Edom shall be a desolate wilderness, for the violence against the children of Judah, because they have shed innocent blood in their land." Joel 3:19 (kjv). "For they know not to do right, saith the LORD, who store up violence and robbery in their palaces. Therefore thus saith the Lord GOD; An adversary there shall be even round about the land; and he shall bring down thy strength from thee, and thy palaces shall be spoiled." Amos 3:10-11 (kjv). "Also to punish the just is not good, nor to strike princes *for equity*." Proverbs 17:26 (kjv) (implying that when princes practice inequity, the people will [eventually] strike the prince).

[361] "I therefore so run, not as uncertainly; so fight I, not as one that beateth the air". 1 Corinthians 9:26 (kjv).

[362] Royal, *Burning The Barn To Roast The Pig? Proportionality Concerns In The War On Terror And The Damadola Incident,* 55.

[363] "'Proportionality contemplates responses parallel in intensity to an initial aggression and designed to discourage future attacks.'" Ibid. at 60, quoting, George K. Walker, The tanker war 1980-88: Law and Policy 150 (U.S. Naval War Coll. Int'l Law studies vol. 84, 2000) supra note 25, at 156.

[364] Ibid. at 55.

[365] Alexander Hamilton, Federalist Paper 8, 61.

[366] Ibid.

[367] Royal, *Burning The Barn To Roast The Pig? Proportionality Concerns In The War On Terror And The Damadola Incident,* 52.

[368] Ibid. at 58.

[369] James Madison, Federalist Paper 51, 400-401.

[370] Alexander Hamilton, Federalist Paper 26, 203.

[371] Alexander Hamilton, Federalist Paper 28, 213.

[372] Alexander Hamilton, Federalist Paper 28, 214 (emphasis added).

[373] Alexander Hamilton, Federalist Paper 28, 215 (emphasis added).

[374] Alexander Hamilton, Federalist Paper 29, 221.

[375] "If one nation maintains constantly a disciplined army, ready for the service of ambition or revenge, it obliges the most pacific nations who may be within the reach of its enterprises to take corresponding precautions." James Madison, Federalist Paper 41, 315.

[376] "The highest number to which, according to the best computation, a standing army can be carried in any country, does not exceed one hundredth part of the whole number of souls; or one twenty-fifth part of the number able to bear arms. This proportion would not yield, in the United States, an army of more than twenty-five or thirty thousand men. To these would be opposed a militia amounting to near half a million of citizens with arms in their hands." James Madison, Federalist Paper 46, 371 (observe, Madison considers every citizen in America to be part of the militia).

[377] "If there should be an army to be made use of as the engine of despotism, what need of the militia?" Alexander Hamilton, Federalist Paper 29, 222.

[378] Alexander Hamilton, Federalist Paper 29, 223.

[379] Alexander Hamilton, Federalist Paper 8, 60.

[380] See, Alexander Hamilton, Federalist Paper 17, discussing the advantage the State will have over the federal government in possessing the support of the people.

[381] Alexander Hamilton, Federalist Paper 29, 221.